SPORTS WRITER'S EYE

Also by Alan Watkins

ALAN WATKINS

SPORTS WRITER'S EYE

AN ANTHOLOGY

Macdonald
Queen Anne Press

A Queen Anne Press Book

First published in Great Britain in 1989 by
Queen Anne Press, a division of
Macdonald & Co (Publishers) Ltd
66-73 Shoe Lane
London EC4P 4AB

A member of Maxwell Pergamon Publishing Corporation plc

British Library Cataloguing in Publication Data
Watkins, Alan
  Sportswriter's eye.
  1. Great Britain. Rugby football, *1981*
  I. Title
  796.33'3'0941

ISBN 0–356–17651–7

Photoset in North Wales by
Derek Doyle & Associates, Mold, Clwyd
Printed and bound in Great Britain by
BPCC Hazell Books Ltd, Aylesbury, Bucks.

CONTENTS

ACKNOWLEDGMENTS

I should like to thank those who commissioned these pieces in the first place: Peter Corrigan and Robert Low, successively sports editor of *The Observer*; Simon Courtauld, then editor of *The Field*; Geoffrey Wheatcroft, then literary and arts editor of *The Spectator*; and Charles Burgess, sports editor of *The Independent*. Further and better particulars about the last three are provided in the separate chapter introductions.

I estimate that I have written over a million and a half words in the last 30 years, excluding books; I ceased keeping my 'cuttings' after about three years, calculating that, if anybody wanted to give me work, he or she would already be familiar with what had already appeared. Accordingly, when a compilation of this kind is being put together, library and secretarial staff are crucial to the enterprise. I should like to thank, for their helpfulness and efficiency in retrieval: Karen Kelner and Jeffrey Care, of *The Observer*; Joanna Stephens, of *The Field*; Julia Mount, of *The Spectator*; and John Hall, of *The Independent*.

All the *Independent* pieces were dictated by telephone from handwritten copy (I write in pen-and-ink on lined foolscap paper). My thanks are due to the copy-taking staff of that paper for their cheerfulness and accuracy. I should also thank the sports sub-editors of the same paper for intervening only to put something right.

Steve Bale, rugby correspondent of *The Independent*, has dealt patiently with various elementary inquiries which I have made of him. His predecessor, Geoffrey Nicholson, who had previously been a colleague of mine on *The Observer*, was unfailingly helpful. Among colleagues my chief debt is, however, owed to Clem Thomas, rugby correspondent of *The Observer*, whose acuity of perception is exceeded only by his generosity of spirit.

Barbara Rieck of *The Observer* typed the introductory sections of this book in her usual impeccable fashion.

My agent, Giles Gordon of Anthony Sheil Associates, pressed me to make progress; while Lorraine Jerram of Queen Anne Press exhibited patience in dealing with a dilatory author. I thank them both.

Alan Watkins

GEOFFREY WHEATCROFT AND OTHERS

In the pieces that follow, there is something about rugby in Scotland, Ireland, France and the Old Commonwealth; a good deal about the game in England; and a great deal about it in Wales. This disproportion may be unsatisfactory to some. It arises not from any principles of selection but from the articles themselves: the whole body of my writing on rugby is skewed not so much in a Welsh as in an Anglo-Welsh direction. This is probably inevitable and, like most preferences or prejudices, goes back a long way.

My father, who appears in some of the pieces that follow, was an elementary schoolmaster teaching in Ammanford and living in Tycroes, respectively a small town and a village in the anthracite area of Carmarthenshire. He started to take me to rugby matches when I was 11 or 12, in 1944–45, at the St Helen's ground, Swansea. Club matches were, of course, suspended owing to the war, but St Helen's put on inter-service matches and service internationals (not to be confused with the Victory Internationals which were played in 1945–46). The teams included players who were already acknowledged as great, such as Lieut Haydn Tanner, and those who already showed the promise of becoming so, such as Pilot Officer Bleddyn Williams. There were former English internationals on display, such as Ray Longland and H. B. Toft, and future internationals, such as Joe Mycock. Above all, there were the Rugby League players, Ernest Ward from England and E. H. (Ted) Ward from Wales. And there was A. J. (Gus) Risman from Wales as well, perhaps the finest of all the backs on display. This accounts for my bias not so much towards Rugby League itself as to a coming together of both codes – a development which, at the amateur level, has begun in the last decade.

After my marriage in 1955 I did not play rugby or even watch it very much. I do not blame my wife for that; there was no grand remonstrance or even any disapproval from her; life changed, that is all. From 1959 to 1964 I was on the staff of the *Sunday Express* and my Saturdays were fully taken up, from 10 in the morning till midnight (Sunday journalists worked longer hours in those days), with leader-writing and other activities. In 1964 I joined *The Spectator* as its political correspondent and, as the work lasted really from Monday morning to Wednesday evening (weekly journalists have usually worked a three-day week, however much they may pretend), I could go to rugby matches again on Saturdays. I even thought of starting to play again – I was then 31 – but a combination of prudence and indolence led me to confine myself to contemplation.

Meanwhile I started to watch London Welsh at Old Deer Park, the club for whom my father had played as a forward 45 years previously, though at Herne Hill in South London rather than at the splendid new ground at Kew. London Welsh were a more impressive outfit than they had been in his own playing days but not by very much: the great days were still to come. John Dawes and Roger Michaelson were already in the team, however. The latter was to create the side of the late 1960s and early 1970s through his ambition and organisational ability; while the former was to become the club's most famous, and the Lions' most successful, captain, even though his later days as an administrator and coach were to belie the promise of his period as a player. But then, why should a good player make a good administrator or coach? My period as a weekly journalist lasted from 1964 to 1976.

In 1967 I had moved to the *New Statesman* to become the political correspondent there. In neither paper was I encouraged to write about rugby. In Iain Macleod's period of editing *The Spectator* (1963–65) I contributed one or two items on the game to the column which he wrote under the pen-name 'Quoodle' (which derived from G.K. Chesterton's lines: 'And Quoodle here discloses, such things as Quoodle can.') This was because Macleod had a genuine liking and some knowledge of rugby, frequently boasting that he never missed a Calcutta Cup match. Otherwise the front half was confined to politics and public affairs generally, and the back half to books and the arts, though even then *The Spectator* had inaugurated the tradition of carrying idiosyncratic and eccentric columns. But sport, certainly rugby, was excluded.

It was the same story at the *New Statesman*, only more so. In the previous couple of decades that fine journalist, Oxford rugby Blue and Labour MP, J. P. W. ('Curly') Mallalieu, had contributed some notable sports articles to the paper, including a few on rugby: but in 1967 we were in a fallow period as far as sportswriting generally was concerned. Certainly the then managing director, Jeremy Potter, thought that sport had no place in the *NS*. This was odd in a way, because Potter, who was very good at the commercial side of his job, was an accomplished club cricketer and hockey-player, and, as often happens with this combination, was adept also at racquets and real tennis. He also wrote detective novels, two of which have hockey and real tennis as their backgrounds. But he did not want sport in the paper.

The editor at that time, Paul Johnson, shared the same opinion, though he possessed a sentimental regard for cricket. Matters changed very slightly when Richard Crossman became editor in 1970. Crossman had played rugby at Oxford, though he had attended a soccer school, Winchester. He had also played, after taking his degree, in a team that included Patrick Gordon Walker and Frank Pakenham (Lord Longford). Unlike these two, however, Crossman evinced little interest in the game in his mature years. The reason the *Statesman* of his day carried the odd article on rugby was that his part-time defence correspondent was Lord Chalfont, formerly Lieutenant-Colonel Alun Gwynne-Jones, a Welshman, a rugby enthusiast and something of an athlete himself.

Crossman's successor, Anthony Howard, was not merely uninterested in sport but positively opposed to it, at any rate in its more aggressive or nationalistic manifestations. However, he had been known to play tennis, and always considered the captain of the England cricket team worthy *ex officio* of a 'profile'. And the *NS* of his period carried several good articles on the business and politics of sport, by Clifford Makins, who had recently ceased being one of the best of *The Observer*'s sports editors, and by Geoffrey Wheatcroft, who had just left his job in publishing to try his hand at freelance journalism.

Wheatcroft was famous for, among other exploits, drawing his unemployment benefit in a morning coat, on his way to Ascot races. We became friends after I moved to Islington in 1974, where he had a flat. A year later he joined the editorial staff of *The Spectator*, becoming literary and arts editor in 1977. Unlike most literary editors, Wheatcroft believed in giving books to people who might write an interesting review rather than to those who were conventionally expert in the general area covered by the work in question. I was sick of writing reviews of *Coketown: A Study of a Typical*

Midlands Seat by R. J. Aaronovitch and Morton Bagel, both of the University of Michigan. Wheatcroft realised this and gave me books to review in which I was more interested. One of them was on rugby and is reprinted here. He also carried the occasional article by me on the game in his arts section.

The article from *The Times*, 'Lloyd-Davies Knew My Father ...', arose because two of the young members of the paper's staff with executive responsibilities, George Brock and Nicholas Wapshott (who was later political editor of *The Observer*), wanted me to write the occasional article for them. They took me out to lunch in Soho, where I explained that the terms of my contract with *The Observer* precluded me from writing about politics for any other paper, but that apart from this I was a free man. I said that I was interested in sport, rugby especially. I was pleased with the Lloyd-Davies piece – he figures later on in this collection – but there was some polite grumbling at *The Observer* at its having appeared on a Saturday, in this case the day of the Wales-England match at Cardiff. It was hazarded that, if this went on regularly, I might be in competition with myself in *The Observer* on the next day. There was no cause for alarm. I was not asked to write again for a long time, and then it was on cricket.

In *The Observer*, in 1978–79, I was writing the back-page 'Pendennis' column in the absence of Michael Davie. I devoted one of my columns to the Raking of Ralston (an episode which is now part of rugby's martyrology, with both sides claiming martyrs). It is reprinted below.

RUGGER'S RUCKUS OVER RUCKING

The Observer, December 1978

In his biography of Dylan Thomas (a good book, even though superseded by Paul Ferris's recent production), Constantine FitzGibbon described Swansea as 'a frontier town'. The description could more aptly be applied to Llanelli, some miles to the west, in what used to be Carmarthenshire, before the 1970 Conservative government changed the name to Dyfed without asking anybody's permission.

For Swansea has always been cosmopolitan, slightly raffish and largely Anglicised: during the last war its evacuees seemed as exotic as those from Acton. Llanelli, on the other hand, is the spot where rural Wales meets and, up to a point, mixes with industrial Wales. It was famous for its tin-plate industry and for its rugby team. The day of the small scale tinworks has gone; the rugby team remains.

The local industry provided the team with one of its two nicknames, 'the Sospans', though the *aficionados* are more likely to refer to it by the other name, 'the Scarlets', after the club's colours. Tin also inspired the club's song, *Sospan Fach*. As the rendering of this number has been known to strike terror into the breasts of visiting touring teams, huddled in their dressing-room under the stand at the club's ground, Stradey Park, it may be worth translating the words: 'Mary Ann's finger has gathered/And David the servant [*that is, the living-in farm labourer*] isn't well/The baby's in the cradle crying/And the cat has scratched little Johnny./Little saucepan boiling on the fire/Big saucepan boiling on the floor. [though some versions repeat the previous line]/And the cat has scratched little Johnny.' There follows a derisive (but neither indecent nor profane) verse about Dai the soldier and some more boastful verses (in English) about beating the Wallabies and the All Blacks, which Llanelli indeed did. The tune is more Russo-Balkan than Welsh; I have heard it played with verve by a Yugoslav band.

The club's supporters are enthusiastic but unpartisan, anxious to applaud the finer points of the game. 'Play football, Llanelli,' is a frequent injunction; meaning not 'kick the ball' but, rather, 'play the game as it ought to be played.'

These supporters are polite to outsiders. I once took a girl, who was English (not that a Welsh girl would have been likely to be more knowledgeable), to see Llanelli play Aberavon. One of the Aberavon players was temporarily laid out flat. 'Oh, poor man,' said the girl. 'I hope he isn't badly hurt.' 'It was the ball that hit him,' a loyal Llanelli supporter explained. 'And what difference is that supposed to make to him?' the girl asked, with a devastating logic which left the supporter quite silent.

Yet Llanelli have never had the reputation of being a dirty or even a particularly rough side. Of course, such reputations vary over the years, depending on the talent available and on the tactics adopted. But, on the whole, Llanelli have been known for open and skilful rugby. Most followers of the game would place them with Cardiff, the Barbarians and Harlequins. There are other clubs – Neath and Pontypool in Wales, Coventry and Gloucester in England – renowned for what is euphemistically known as 'power play'. The New Zealanders are likewise famous for it.

Nor is it a coincidence that, while Llanelli have produced some great forwards since the last war alone – Delme Thomas, Rhys Williams and Derek Quinnell, for instance – the folk heroes have been backs, men of obvious skills. There was Albert Jenkins before the war; after it, Terry Davies, Terry Price, Lewis Jones, Phil Bennett and, above all, Barry John.

This may help put in perspective the events of 4 November at the Richmond Athletic Ground. Llanelli were playing Richmond. Chris Ralston, the former England and British Lions forward, was tackled by a Llanelli forward and put the ball back towards his own line, as is the approved practice. The forwards that remained, a maximum of seven on each side, then tore into one another and tried to heel or hook the ball with backward motions of the feet. This is again the approved practice in modern rugby. It is known as a ruck or, as the jargon has it, 'a ruck-situation'. As Clem Thomas has already pointed out several times in *The Observer*, the practice is by its nature dangerous if there is a man or men on the ground, as is virtually inevitable.

At all events, Ralston sustained two parallel horizontal wounds on the forehead and scalp. He went off the field, a replacement for him came on and the game continued without further untoward incident. Indeed, in the dressing room after the match, where champagne was produced by the match's sponsors, tribute was paid to the excellent spirit in which the game had been played, typical of encounters between Richmond and Llanelli, and so forth. At this stage the extent of Ralston's injuries, which required over 30 stitches, was not known by either side. At about 5.15 the Llanelli team left the Richmond clubhouse to catch the 6.15 train to Wales.

According the one Press report, Richmond's indignation over Ralston's injuries grew with every pint consumed – Llanelli were by now on the train – during the rest of Saturday evening. This is quoted with some relish in the town of Llanelli. But whether it is so or not, it is the case that Llanelli players and officials first learned of the scale of the episode on the following Monday. (In 'officials' I include team advisers who are not technically club officials.)

On this day it was clear that Llanelli had a major rugby row on their hands. Ralston himself said in essence three things: first, that the injury was deliberate; second, that he knew who had done it; and, third, that he contemplated taking legal action against the offender. The first name to crop up was that of Charles Thomas the prop-forward. Thomas subsequently denied all in the Press on the general lines of: 'I am not a villain, says Charles Thomas.'

Oddly, however, the Richmond club named Llanelli a different culprit, the other Llanelli prop-forward, John Williams (not to be confused with J. J. Williams, the Llanelli and Welsh wing, or J. P. R. Williams, the Welsh full-back). But it was later established by Llanelli that it was Williams who had originally tackled Ralston. Of all the 16 forwards on both sides, he and Ralston were the indisputably guiltless men. And in the investigation that followed, it was Ralston's promise or threat of legal action which assumed the greatest importance. It has always been possible for one player,

8

whether of rugby or any other game, to sue another for injury inflicted outside the rules of the game. Though there were isolated examples in the law reports, the general view was that this aspect of the law of tort was something of an academic joke.

No longer. With the increasing violence of most sports, especially perhaps rugby, several players have taken successful action. Anyway, as one Llanelli official put it: 'The lads were scared out of their wits by the threat of being taken to court. After all, they're mainly quite young.'

It is unnecessary to record all the details of the successive meetings involving the club's coach (John Maclean), the management committee, the captain (Bennett) and most of the forwards concerned. The club's solicitor, Alan Jenkins, was also brought into the affair, understandably enough. There are two crucial points. The decision was made to confront the forwards collectively. And all eight forwards could not be gathered together until 12 days after the initial event. This may seem surprising but one has to take the club's word for it. A few days before this gathering Llanelli had suspended all eight forwards. This was just before the match with Swansea, which Llanelli won with a fresh pack. The suspension caused astonishment everywhere and elicited an approving article in the *Daily Telegraph*, which paid tribute to rugby as a game played by gentlemen of every class.

Llanelli claimed that this suspension was a brave, indeed unprecedented, act which demonstrated their *bona fides* and determination to arrive at the truth. In retrospect it may have been a political error. For a few days later the eight forwards were for the first time gathered together, and the injuries to Ralston found to have been an accident. Now this was by no means a ridiculous finding. Injuries such as those to Ralston could have been caused accidentally not merely by Llanelli but even by Richmond players. However, the suspension of eight forwards inevitably led to the expectation that one of them would finally be named. When none was, there was the equally inevitably cry of 'whitewash'.

The word 'accidental' is ambiguous. Does it mean: 'We know who did it but we're not telling because he didn't intend to injure Ralston'? Or: 'We don't know who did it and we're satisfied it was an accident'? Llanelli officials maintain the latter. Well, they would, wouldn't they? is the cynical response. And it is one that arouses anger. The Richmond club and the English rugby correspondents (the favourite Llanelli hate-figures of the moment) are using the original suspension of the eight forwards as evidence of typical Welsh cunning. In fact, the officials say, the suspension was a sincere effort to arrive at the truth. 'There are no known villains in the Llanelli pack,' one official said. 'I sometimes wish there were.'

As it happens, the technique of driving over the man with the feet in an effort to win the ball, was largely brought to Britain by Carwyn James, the great Llanelli and British Lions coach, now coaching in Italy. Once a ruck has formed it is illegal to handle the ball. Clem Thomas has suggested that the laws should be changed to allow handling. Rubber, as distinct from plastic or aluminium, studs in the boots might also help to diminish the number of injuries.

Change will amost certainly be opposed in New Zealand, the home of rucking. In the present controversy Richmond wait for Llanelli to do something. And Llanelli wait for Richmond. Earlier this season a Welsh player died after his neck was broken in a scrum collapse. A few more deaths will probably be necessary before anything is actually done about the dangerous state of rugby.

STRAIGHTFORWARD
The Spectator, February 1980

The only piece of advice Sir (as he now is) Ian Gilmour gave me when he was proprietor of *The Spectator*, and I its political correspondent, was that it was 'bad journalism' to say 'as I write' or 'at the time of writing'. The art of the weekly, as distinct from the daily or Sunday, trade – so Sir Ian opined – was to make what had been written on the Tuesday appear up-to-date when it arrived at Scunthorpe on the Saturday, if, indeed, it arrived there at all. There had to be some sleight of hand. No doubt this was good advice; I tried to follow it as best I could; but there are times when the direct approach is preferable.

So: as I write, the Welsh team for the match at Twickenham on 16 February is unannounced. Wales have the problem of whether to bring in Peter Morgan and Derek Quinnell, both of Llanelli, in place of Roger Blyth and Eddie Butler at full-back and No 8 respectively. Quinnell was injured before the French match; the position of Morgan was more doubtful. Though this problem – or, rather, these two problems – will have been resolved by the time this is read, the matter is still worth some discussion. For it is a sign of triviality of mind to be interested only in results or conclusions, at the expense of what went before.

When Quinnell arrived in New Zealand in 1971 with the British Lions, he was uncapped by Wales. The New Zealanders considered him one of the best forwards in the world. Since then he has won 22 Welsh caps: but he has never found a secure place, mainly because, to begin with, he oscillated between lock and flanker. Then with Mervyn Davies's retirement he was turned into a No 8, but he is now getting on, and is none too quick on his pins. (His replacement in the French match, Butler, struck a blow for normality and common sense in being six foot two and 14½ stone: the pundits shook their heads and said 'too small', but he did well enough.)

With Morgan the Llanelli club have behaved differently – though what has happened this season may have been by his own choice. For when the message went out from the Welsh selectors that Quinnell was to be Davies's successor at No 8, Llanelli regularly played him in that position, so displacing Hefin Jenkins, who had himself once been on the margin of the Welsh side. Morgan, by contrast, has been flitting between full-back, centre and outside-half – mainly between the last two positions – even though he was supposed to be J. P. R. Williams's successor as the Welsh full-back.

But Wales have usually had a surplus of players of this

11

kind. Bryan Richards, Carwyn James and J. D. Bevan, among outside-halves of the last couple of decades, were all unlucky not to win more caps. Gareth Davies now seems set for the next decade, and the Welsh selectors have acknowledged this by putting David Richards into the centre. The Irish selectors, by contrast, do not seem inclined to play Tony Ward either at centre or at full-back, now that Ollie Campbell has arrived. I hope the Lions selectors show more sense, and pick all five of them, however they may be distributed on paper in the team announcement: Davies, Richards, Morgan, Ward and Campbell.

If John Horton of England carries on as at present, he will be in with a chance of the South Africa trip too. For the first revelation of the season is that the England midfield can perform competently. The second revelation is that the Welsh midfield can perform not only competently (this we knew) but magnificently – that Davies, above all, is a runner as well as a kicker and passer. The third revelation ... but this is not really a revelation at all. For the last decade and more there has been agreement in the clubhouses, Welsh as well as English, that, potentially, England have the best pack in the five countries.

It is not that the nucleus of the present pack has been neglected or gone unrewarded: Peter Wheeler, Fran Cotton, Bill Beaumont, Roger Uttley and Tony Neary possess great experience. But in the past they were not kept together, partly through injury (especially to Cotton and Uttley) and partly through the vagaries of selection. In particular, Cotton was not chosen in his preferred position of loose-head prop. Even so, the England pack did enough in previous seasons to win more matches than they in fact won. They were let down by the English backs: not so much by their running as by their reluctance to run. Now that England have a lively midfield in Horton, Nick Preston and Clive Woodward, it seems not only illogical but depressing for such observers as John Reason of the *Sunday Telegraph* to urge a return to the (his phrase) snowplough centre.

SELECTED

The Spectator, March 1980

Before the announcement of the Lions team, Donald Trelford, the editor of *The Observer*, and I made a bet: whichever nominated the larger number of those selected would win. Trelford won by 25 to 23. He was right about Tomes and Gravell. He was wrong about Rees, Dodge, Orr, Leslie and Scott. I was wrong about Rees, Dodge, Orr, G. Roberts (Swansea), Gibson, McLennon and Wheel.

All in all, a creditable performance by *The Observer*. The player, we agreed, to whom the greatest injustice had been done was Tony Ward of Ireland. He ought surely to have been in there somewhere, though we both predicted that he would not find favour with the selectors. I was myself influenced by the possibility that there would be an anti-Welsh movement: hence the omission on my part of Gravell, Quinnell and Clive Williams. No one can really criticise the selectors for what they have done. No one also can deny Bill Beaumont part of the credit for England's success this season. He deserves the leadership of the Lions XV.

The season produced much good rugby; especially in the game between England and Scotland last Saturday; but it will be remembered for the match between England and Wales at Twickenham. Paul Ringer of Llanelli should, some commentators thought, have been dropped from the side who met England. I myself believed that Ringer ought to have been given a firm talking-to before the match. In the event none of this happened, and Ringer was quite rightly sent off for his short-arm tackle on Horton.

There is no point in disguising the fact that the England v Wales match was, though not the paradigmatic match of the season, nevertheless the match which people will remember. Some Welshmen said that, in regard to the sending-off of Ringer, the event had been decided beforehand; others said that this game accounted for the meiotic performance of the Welsh forwards in the games against both Scotland and Ireland. The Welsh excuses abound.

What few have so far done is to arrive at some position whereby violence in Rugby Union can be diminished. There have been proposals for replacing aluminium studs, which can form sharp edges, with plastic studs. Teams have rejected these proposals. There have been other proposals as well. Few Rugby Union players wish the game to be like Rugby League, where the ruck and the maul are abolished, but Clem Thomas in *The Observer* has long urged that handling should be permitted in the ruck. There seems little consciousness among rugby administrators of the need to change, and the current state of good spirits in English rugby circles, following the Grand Slam, the championship and Beaumont's nomination to the Lions captaincy, should not divert supporters from the real problems which this season, perhaps above all others, has presented.

A LAND AND ITS GAME

The Spectator, November 1980

An Autobiography David Watkins (Cassell, £6.95)
Welsh Rugby: The Crowning Years 1968–80 Clem Thomas and Geoffrey Nicholson (Collins, £6.95)
A Touch of Glory Alun Richards (Michael Joseph, £8.50)
The Illustrated History of Welsh Rugby J. B. G. Thomas (Pelham, £10.50)
Decade of the Dragon John Taylor (Hodder, £7.95)
Fields of Praise David Smith and Gareth Williams (University of Wales, £12.95)

The 1970s saw more books on rugby published than any previous decade; and this year, the centenary of the Welsh Rugby Union, shows that publishers are just as alive to the commercial opportunities of this commemoration as the WRU itself. Still, all the books under consideration have their points of interest.

David Watkins was a marvellous outside-half who just missed a great era, but who made the transition to Rugby

League more successfully than any recent player except Lewis Jones. Clem Thomas and Geoffrey Nicholson (from Swansea likewise) are two of our best rugby journalists, Thomas writing with unrivalled experience and authority, and Nicholson possessing a gift of phrase that few reporters can match. J. B. G. Thomas consolidates his position as the most prolific rugby writer in the history of the world. John Taylor, in an invaluable book, tells us what it was like to be in the Welsh team of the 1970s, which, with all the other players' autobiographies, must by now be the best-documented rugby period of all time. Alun Richards, in a book based on a television series, gives us a short, readable history of Welsh rugby. David Smith and Gareth Williams provide a longer history which is a minor masterpiece.

Mr Smith and Mr Williams are academic historians; both born in 1945, both Welsh, both at Balliol for a time, both rugby enthusiasts. Their book was commissioned by the WRU. It could have turned out very differently. It could have been a history of the organisation, with much detail about committees and sub-committees. The authors tell us about this kind of thing, but only as much as we need to know to understand the story. There is another error to which Welsh writers on Welsh matters are prone. This is to combine sentimentality with boastfulness of a silly sort, on the lines of 'the Tudors were Welsh, and so was Oliver Cromwell, not to mention Christopher Columbus.' There is an accompanying tendency to suppress wit or humour of a self-depreciatory nature for fear of being thought 'anti-Welsh'. From this last fault Mr Smith and Mr Williams are wholly free.

Welsh rugby was a product of the last quarter of the 19th century, when south Wales turned into something like the Klondyke. Merthyr had been industrialised well before this, and Swansea was already an important metallurgical centre: but on the whole the industrial revolution came late to Wales. Mr Smith and Mr Williams rightly emphasise not the hardship but the sense of opportunity. Indeed (though our authors do not express it in so many words) south Wales before 1914 was not the industrial slum that was later to be romanticised by popular novelists and patronised by English public schoolboys with pretensions to communism. The anthracite miners of Carmarthenshire, for instance, often owned solid, stone-built, detached houses with large gardens. Cardiff and Swansea were fine cities.

Inevitably there were tensions caused by the immigration of Scotsmen, Irishmen, West Countrymen and Welshmen from rural Wales. Mr Smith and Mr Williams pay lip service to the theory of rugby as 'social control'. I put it so because I do not feel they are wholly convinced of it themselves. But certainly industrialists encouraged the new sport whose importation had owed much to West Countrymen. The other encouraging influence was the Anglican Church (later to be disestablished as the Church in Wales). St David's College, Lampeter, an anomalous institution which supplied most of the Welsh clergy, was prominent in the formation of the Welsh Football Union. Later, forwards of the early years of this century such as the Rev. Glyn Stephens (father of Rees), the Rev. Alban Davies and the Rev. W. T. Havard were to demonstrate that the church militant was no mere idle phrase.

The chapels, by contrast, were suspicious of the new game, as they remained until recently. Similarly, the cultural leaders of Welsh-speaking rural Wales were hostile: they began to be less so only when they realised that prowess at rugby could be exploited for their own nationalistic purposes.

Evan Roberts's religious revival of 1905 bowled over clubs and players: 'At Ynysybwl, the entire team was baptised and all sporting activities were rejected for three years. After hearing Evan Roberts preach at Kenfig Hill, veteran footballer Jenkin Thomas announced to a startled congregation, "I used to play full-back for the devil, but now I'm forward for God." In west Wales rugby was suspended at Morriston, Penygroes and Crynant for four years. The revival killed off rugby in Evan Roberts's home town of Loughor till 1909; it "spelt doom to Ammanford rugby" till 1907.'

The revival apart, the authors attribute the hostility of the chapels to gambling on matches and to the fact that clubs frequently had their headquarters in public houses – that in any case beer was part of the game. My own feeling is that they underestimate the puritan objection to pleasure and to any activity coming between man and his creator.

In Wales all conflicts are cross-conflicts and rugby was no exception. The conflict was not only between chapel and pub but between east and west. The saying 'To get a cap you've got to go to Cardiff' was current in west Wales as recently as 20 years ago; even 10 years ago, three great players from the Swansea-Llanelli catchment area, Barry John, Gareth Edwards and Gerald Davies, attained fame with Cardiff; likewise Gareth Davies today. On the other hand, the late 1960s saw the migration of players such as J. J. Williams and Tom David to Llanelli. In the 1920s the Llanelli club felt persecuted. The reason was the persistent ignoring by the selectors of Albert Jenkins, who, it was felt with some justification, was the finest centre of his time. Jenkins was famous not only for his playing prowess but for his consumption of beer, his illiteracy (though this is disputed by some) and his general good nature.

The argument quickly turned from one of geography to one of class: the Welsh selectors, it was opined in Llanelli, were preferring 'college boys', especially from Cambridge, among the backs. The heroes of the pre-1914 period had, on the whole, been working men. In the inter-war period the tendency was to choose working-class forwards and Oxbridge backs. The proportion of miners was always exaggerated by those who took an impressionistic view, and that of policemen underestimated, though not by Mr Smith and Mr Williams. However, I should have liked some detailed occupational analyses.

I should also have liked some breakdown of average heights and weights in comparison to other countries: this because until recently one common view in Wales was that the team could not properly exploit its talents because the forwards were too small. Accordingly, Welsh success since the mid-1960s is to be explained by improved diet and general standard of life. The authors lend no support to this view: the inter-war forwards, they say, were big enough but (with numerous exceptions) unskilful. The recent spell of success was due not to orange juice but to gifted individuals, to the success of teams like Bridgend, Llanelli and London Welsh and, above all, to coaching.

The authors do tend to become a little organisational on coaching, but this is, I suppose, inevitable. On the whole one can only admire their skill in linking match reports with short biographies of famous players, profiles of clubs with accounts of the finances of the WRU. They stand up, I am glad to see, for the old Welsh rugby truths: that the game is there not to form character but to provide a means of self-expression; that supporting a team is every bit as strenuous and morally worthy as actually playing; and that, in a free country, the referee must expect a bit of adverse criticism from time to time.

LLOYD-DAVIES KNEW MY FATHER ...
The Times, February 1983

There was no television in those days. If you wanted to see the international, you had to go there. For the England and Wales match, as for all internationals, my father always wore his best suit. He also wore a hat, a heavy overcoat, leather gloves and, depending on the weather, a silk or woollen scarf. Though he was by no means sympathetic to communism – quite the reverse – the general effect of his outfit was to make him resemble a large but politically obscure member of the Politburo who was about to take the salute at a parade of tanks. In fact he was a Welsh schoolmaster who, while neither vain nor pushful, felt he had standards to maintain. He would no more have gone to the match with a leek and a red and white scarf than he would have appeared in front of his class with a false nose. I was expected to be correctly attired likewise, even if less splendidly.

The first match we saw together was not, strictly speaking, an international. It was the Victory International of 1946 for which no full caps were awarded. We travelled from Tycroes in Carmarthenshire to Cardiff in a hired single-decker bus (there were few coaches then). Also on the bus was another son of the village, Hugh Lloyd-Davies, in his pilot officer's uniform, who was playing for Wales at full-back.

Lloyd-Davies was an exciting though unpredictable performer who, a year later, was to win the university match for Cambridge by kicking two penalty goals. On this occasion he did not have the happiest of afternoons. Two pre-war English players, Jack Heaton and Dickie Guest, both of Waterloo, effectively won the match for England, Heaton with his cross-kicking and Guest with his elusiveness. Indeed, Guest was a wing in the class of Peter Jackson or Gerald Davies who, but for the war, would surely have won more than his 13 caps. He twice went round Lloyd-Davies to score.

We could see because we were standing by that right-hand corner flag. Despite my father's correctness of dress and demeanour, we never sat in the stand but always stood in the 'field' or the somewhat superior 'enclosure': partly because stand tickets were hard to come by, partly, I suspect, because my father did not believe in throwing his money around and partly, I suspect also, because he would have considered it 'spoiling' to show me relative luxury at too early an age.

After the match we came on Lloyd-Davies, now back in his RAF uniform, behind the stand. My father, an old London Welsh forward of the years immediately after the First World War (though he would emphasise, that he had been 'lucky to get into the team'), was stern with the young full-back. 'I could see,' he said, 'that you were looking at his face, not his legs. It was his legs that went round you, not his face,' he added, to leave no misunderstanding about his views on correct play by a full-back.

At this and subsequent matches, we had a ritual. We did not eat before the match, but afterwards had a substantial tea. The menu was unchanging and suited the tastes of both of us. We had fish and chips, cakes (or 'pastries' as my father called them) and a pot of tea. He was always emphatic with the waitress about the need for a pot of tea; a cup each was not good enough. Thus fortified, we would walk to the headquarters hotel. This was almost certainly the most important part of the day for my father and partly accounted

19

for his best suit. He was able to enter the hotel with confidence not so much because of any renown as an old player (he was, as I have said, modest about his past abilities) as because of his friendship with Aneurin Jenkins, a Cardiff schoolmaster and a member of the Cardiff Rugby Club.

Jenkins was by now a widower with no immediate family who lived in lodgings: the Cardiff club was not only his home but virtually his life. Like many of his type, he took a keen, even obsessive interest in rugby politics. He was a great obtainer of tickets, forecaster of selections, nodder and winker and putter of fingers to the nose. He knew not only players, members of the great post-war Cardiff side, but also administrators, even the selectors, 'the Big Five' themselves.

The year after the Victory International was that of the first full post-war match between England and Wales. This was also a time of one of the great recurring Welsh outside-half controversies. It was not simple. Should the outside-half be Glyn Davies of Pontypridd, later of Cambridge University, one of the classic, darting Welsh outside-halves? Or should it be the more utilitarian Billy Cleaver of Cardiff, 'Billy Kick' as he was called in west Wales?

But this choice did not exhaust the dispute. For there was Bleddyn Williams, also of Cardiff, to consider. Bleddyn was acknowledged to be a great centre-three-quarter even then. But might he not turn out to be an even greater outside-half? In other words, was outside-half Bleddyn's true position? Or was it not? On this occasion, in 1947, the selectors decided it was. Bleddyn played outside the equally great Haydn Tanner, with Cleaver and Jack Matthews, also of Cardiff, in the centre. This combination was known in the public prints as 'the Cardiff triangle'. It was widely expected to beat England on its own. Alas, it failed. Bleddyn suffered a muscle strain in the first few minutes and, though Wales scored two tries to England's one, Wales lost because the late Nim Hall dropped a goal.

Afterwards Jenkins, my father and I were sitting in the lounge of the hotel. Two Welsh forwards, Rees Stephens of Neath and George Parsons of Newport, had somehow attached themselves to our party – or we had attached ourselves to them. Quite what these young men made of having to converse with two middle-aged schoolmasters and a 13-year-old boy with a balaclava helmet was difficult to say, but they were civil enough. Then Jenkins espied one of the selectors, David Jones (Blaina), who was always called 'David Jones (Blaina)'. Jenkins invited him over. 'So the mighty triangle didn't come off,' my father said to him. 'We live and learn,' said David Jones (Blaina).

Thirty-six years later, however, I shall not be mingling with the great. I shall be sitting before the television set, not wearing my best suit.

2

SIMON COURTAULD AND OTHERS

'Thus ... we come up against a factor which will reappear constantly in this book – the advantage of being personally known to those in key positions. I do not propose to moralise about this; it is just another element in the literary profession which aspirant literateurs must foresee and make allowance for, and if they don't like it they should go elsewhere (only to find, of course, that the same conditions obtain).' – Simon Raven, *Boys Will Be Boys*, 1963.

Readers of the introduction to Section 1 will have noted that I started to write about rugby in *The Spectator* because Geoffrey Wheatcroft was appointed literary and arts editor of that paper. It was a change in the higher command of the same paper which led to my second tour of duty as a rugby writer, with *The Field*. In 1984 Alexander Chancellor resigned as editor after a disagreement with the then proprietor, J. G. ('Algy') Cluff, and departed to the *Sunday Telegraph*. Chancellor's deputy, Simon Courtauld, left simultaneously, as is often the way when editors change, and after a few months was appointed editor of *The Field*. Courtauld had, unlike me, briefly practised as a barrister. He had also held the position of managing director at *The Spectator* together with that of deputy editor. He was a good cricketer and looked like an army officer. He bore a striking resemblance to the Duke of Kent. He was of the well-known Huguenot family.

The Field had traditionally confined itself more to strictly rural pursuits, notably hunting, shooting and fishing, than had its rival, *Country Life*, which ranged more widely, particular attention being paid to domestic architecture. Its articles on the last were, indeed, often cited in biographies and in works of scholarship. Courtauld wanted to widen the appeal of *The Field* also, but in slightly different directions. He wanted to include more general articles by writers who were professional or well-known or, preferably, both. He recruited Gillian Widdicombe to write on music, William Deedes on golf, Geoffrey Wheatcroft on racing, John McEwen on art, me on rugby, and Jo Grimond, Peter Paterson and Alec Home on whatever came into their heads. None of us was *outré*. Indeed, some of us would, I suspect, have appealed to the paper's old readers. But we were a mixed bunch all the same. What they made of us I do not know.

I dealt chiefly with Jeremy Alexander, who had come from *The Guardian*, knew a lot about soccer but was by no means ignorant of rugby, saving me from error on several occasions. There was also a talented young sub-editor called David Jones who wrote occasionally in *The Spectator* under the name Lewis Jones because he thought that it sounded more impressive and that there were too many David Joneses in the world anyway. The secretaries looked as if they had enjoyed a morning's hacking and, the office being near Blackfriars station, were conveniently placed to catch the District or Circle line to South Kensington or Sloane Square.

The *Observer* office, in which I then appeared for three mornings a week, was placed equally conveniently from my own point of view, a few hundred yards away on the City side of Blackfriars. Once a fortnight, at the beginning of the week, I would take my copy across New Bridge Street to *The Field*'s offices in Carmelite Street, by the *Daily Mail*. The offices were in a pre-1914 building, all tiles, shiny linoleum and polished brasswork, with one of those lifts with metal grilles in which I always fear I am going to crush my fingers. The uniformed commissionaires appeared to have come with the building, concealing beneath their forced deference indolence and inefficiency which were remarkable. Copy marked 'copy' would be delivered in three or four hours, whereas copy marked 'urgent copy' would be in the editor's hands next day. The trick was to say who you were, to walk upstairs past their disapproving looks and to deliver the column personally to Courtauld or one of his young assistants.

It was too good to last; nor did it. The magazine was owned by Associated Newspapers which had – the word is like a knell to any journalist – 'plans' for it. First it was transformed into a monthly from having been a weekly (even though my rugby column had appeared only fortnightly). I thought as a partial outsider that this was a sensible move which was in tune with the character of the magazine. Naturally it worked to a monthly – even seasonal – view of the world. Simon Courtauld did not see matters in this light and was upset. So were his staff. They turned out to be right. The change was the beginning of the end for Courtauld's *Field*. Shortly afterwards it became a 'lifestyle' magazine emphasising the 'concept' of country living. Courtauld left for, eventually, another magazine. But, well before then, I had left *The Field*, to start a rugby column on *The Independent*.

TEAMS LOVED AND UNLOVED
The Field, December 1984

Scotland ended last season in much the same position as the one in which the Arsenal Football Club has often found itself.

It had won everything. Its players, or some of them, had been quite distinguished. And yet it was somehow unloved, unappreciated, neglected. Lucky Arsenal, lucky Scotland! Why, the question went, are you outsiders so ungenerous to us? We have, Scotsmen said, the best front row in Milne, Deans and Aitken. At least the first two should have been regulars for the Lions. We also have the best back row in Calder, Paxton and Leslie. All three should have been with the Lions – in fact Leslie, the best of the lot, was not even on the trip to New Zealand. We furthermore have the best, or anyway most consistent, pair of half-backs in Rutherford and Laidlaw.

To which one can only murmur: quite so, quite so, but don't worry, please, because you did win last season, after all, and on the evidence of this season so far you may win again. Scotland was not in fact that famous blend of youth and experience, which some assume to be required. Most of the players had been around for a long time. The combination suddenly worked.

Ireland's combination worked a few seasons ago. It did not work last season. This time the selectors have come up with a new lot which, with the pressure of time, they had no choice but to do. Their performance against Australia was, to me, excellent. I cannot understand why some of my colleagues in the Press have, in relation to the same opposition, bracketed them with sad England and even sadder Wales. Perhaps the team illustrated no more than the traditional Irish virtues of chasing everything that moved and tackling everyone irrespective of whether he moved or not. But they certainly illustrated those virtues impressively.

Michael Kiernan and Moss Finn remain two of the most penetrative three-quarters in British rugby. I have one doubt, however. It may seem a strength that they have now switched between centre and wing, with Kiernan the old centre as new wing, Finn the old wing as new centre. It shows adaptability, versatility and the rest. Sometimes such changes can work marvellously. One can instance Gerald Davies's move (to the initial displeasure of the Welsh selectors) from the centre to wing in the 1960s. But more often these changes leave players

– or, more important perhaps, selectors – not knowing where they are. A few years ago Llanelli had a particularly gifted set of young backs, some of them still playing: Kevin Thomas, David Nicholas, Martin Gravelle, Peter Morgan. They all lost through being switched around. Still, I wish Kiernan and Finn well. I am not sure that I wish the Irish selectors quite so much good fortune if they continue in their madness of omitting, in Ollie Campbell's absence, Tony Ward – even though they had a typical piece of Irish luck in the Australian match when Kiernan proved the equal of Ward.

But everybody loves Ireland, while nobody loves poor old England. It is more unloved than Scotland even. This is not the place to enter into yet another discussion of counties and clubs, divisions and merit tables. It is enough for the moment to observe that England possesses a potentially fine full-back in Stuart Barnes but that he prefers to play – anyway plays – at stand-off half; that Rob Andrew of Cambridge University is an exciting stand-off half; that there are at least four and possibly more wings of Lions standard; that to permute virtually any two from Salmon, Thompson, Dodge, Woodward and Simms, to name but a few (though quite enough to be going on with), would give England a better pair of centres than the two who played against Australia; that the Gloucestershire props with Steve Brain between them would serve well enough; that England is blessed with a luxury of talent in the back row; and that it all turns to sackcloth and ashes, so to speak.

Poor old Wales, too. At the end of last season I thought that many of my fellow countrymen were being unreasonably optimistic, largely on the strength of the team's – particularly Malcolm Dacey's – performance against England. Yet it was obvious even then that the somewhat makeshift back row of Moriarty, Butler and Pickering was not quite up to it and that there were other areas of fragility as well. Nevertheless I thought Wales would beat Australia. Perhaps the defeat should not have come as quite the shock it did. For the banned Moriarty, himself a made-up flanker, the selectors introduced another of the big, improvised variety: Alun Davies of Llanelli, who had played most of his previous rugby as a very ordinary club No 8 and had, owing to illness, played only three times during the season.

John Bevan, the coach, again continued to give Dacey preference over Gareth Davies because of Dacey's running capabilities (though Davies is not actually immobile). The decision having been made, the selectors absurdly chose as scrum-half an exponent, in David Bishop of Pontypool, not so much of 10-man as of nine-man and often one-man rugby. Bishop believes in the elbow-off rather than the hand-off. In scoring his try he did not make a 'readjustment': the ball went yards forward. His egotistical performance was, I thought, treated overindulgently by the commentators.

Clearly Wales's best half-backs are Davies and, in the continuing absence of Holmes, Mark Douglas of London Welsh, formerly of Llanelli. Douglas has had some mediocre games this season. He can still pass the ball certainly longer and probably faster than Bishop. But then, a player going from a Welsh club to London Welsh is treated much as a foreign correspondent going from Washington to Bonn. It is somehow thought he has disappeared from view.

I hope to write about France in another column, which will, I trust, be more cheerful – from the French point of view anyway.

FOR LOVE OR MONEY
The Field, January 1985

A few years ago an acquaintance of mine, who was also on the committee of a leading London club, asked me whether I knew anyone in the brewing business. I replied that my relationship with brewers was that of customer rather than friend – more commercial than personal. In any case, why was he asking? Well, you see, there was this English international, who had been working and playing in France, and now wanted to return to England. He was prepared to play for this London club if it would provide him with a house to live in and a pub to manage. The house, my committeeman acquaintance implied, could be arranged easily enough. The pub presented greater difficulties. Hence the inquiry about my connections, if any, with brewers. (The player concerned, I may add, was not Maurice Colclough.)

As things turned out, the English international played a few times for another London club, which presumably enjoyed a greater influence in the brewing trade than the one to which my acquaintance belonged. He then disappeared from the rugby scene. He was, in any case, approaching the end of his career.

From this little story no one emerges with any discredit, provided one assumption is granted. That assumption is that rugby is more than an amateur game. The player, quite straightforwardly, wanted somewhere to live and a particular kind of job to do. The club was anxious to secure his services and was accordingly equally concerned to meet his wishes. Similar arrangements are entered into every day. 'Executives' receive help with their mortgages and removal expenses. Journalists posted to foreign parts have their accommodation found, their rent paid. Complicated calculations are made about exchange rates, rules laid down about what may or may not be charged as expenses.

But arrangements of this kind are entered into in an openly commercial context. To find someone a house is to do him a service, irrespective of whether he subsequently pays the rent or mortgage himself. To find someone a job is, in effect, to provide him with money, irrespective of whether he subequently works for that money. Yet rugby clubs will continue to entice players with offers of houses and jobs. If this practice is contrary to the laws (which is arguable either way, I should have thought), no amount of enforcement is going to change it.

There are really three separate questions which rugby men have to settle but tend to be muddled up. The first question – if rugby is to stay a more or less amateur game – is about how amateurism is to be interpreted so that the result is fair, realistic and without humbug. The second is whether rugby should stay an amateur game at all. And the third concerns the way the Rugby Unions should conduct themselves towards the Rugby League. Perhaps it is a little strong for me to write that these questions 'have to' be settled. In this world you do not *have* to do anything except pay your income tax and die. In any case, I know that these questions will see most of us out and stay largely unanswered. What I really mean is that they will not go away and that we should try to answer them for the sake of our self-respect, if for no other reason.

The 'boot money scandal' seems to have gone away because the authorities claimed that there was a paucity of evidence. In fact there was only too much evidence. They preferred not to consider it. The question of relations between Union and League is very much with us, with the threat of Ray French, the League television commentator (and former international in both codes), to take the Union to court over its purported prohibition of his coaching schoolboys.

But this question is, as I say, separate from that of amateurism. Here the principle is, or should be, clear enough. No one should be paid, in cash or kind, for playing rugby. Alas, it breaks down in practice, as principles are prone to do. It does not break down at all over the writing of books. A player or former player who writes a book is being paid not for playing rugby but for writing a book – or having a book written on his behalf. To suggest otherwise is to be insulting both to writers and to rugby players. The present rule is not only illogical. It is also applied inconsistently. The New Zealander Andy Haden writes a 'controversial' book – not that whether it is controversial affects the principle of the thing – and is allowed to carry on playing as if nothing had happened. The Welshman J. P. R. Williams writes a book and is allowed to retain his amateur status because the proceeds of sale go towards research on sports injuries. (Would the decision have been the same, I wonder, if he had given the proceeds to, say, the BMA?) The Scotsman Ian McLauchlan writes a book and is consigned to the dark regions.

Then there is the matter of expenses. 'No one was ever out of pocket playing for Swansea,' a committeeman of that club said a few years ago. Whereupon a knowing laugh went up all the way from Stradey Park to Richmond Park. For Welsh clubs are renowned, or notorious, for their generosity to their players.

And yet the principle of not being out of pocket is sound enough. It breaks down only with the 'broken-time' which itself led to the setting up of the Northern League – the payment of money in lieu of wages that would otherwise have been earned. In logic this is no doubt an expense: in practice it is a wage. But I doubt whether even the most generous payment of legitimate expenses is going to satisfy players. Not long before he died last year, Ricky Bartlett said to me that semi-professionalism on League lines was bound to come in the end. He added that he would not play under present conditions, with all the training and travel, unless he were paid something.

I think Bartlett would have played just the same. But he was right in saying that more was expected of players today. Perhaps it would be better if players reverted in some respects to the methods of Bartlett's day, and practised accurate kicking, for example, instead of trying to turn themselves into SAS desperadoes: but that is another subject. The immediate point is that players are now expected to work hard. Not only that: they see money coming into the game through television and commercial sponsorship and see no reason why they should not have a share of it. The would-be Packer figure who appeared on the scene a few years ago was somewhat farcical, to be sure. But some day a real Packer is going to turn up, and the rugby authorities will be as unprepared as the cricket authorities were. Their idea of purposeful action is to keep their heads down and to continue to persecute Rugby League – and its representatives such as Ray French.

CARWYN AND THE WELSH CHORUS
The Field, January 1985

Alun Richards has been on my conscience for a long time; four years, to be exact. In 1980, the centenary of the Welsh Rugby Union, he published a short history of the game in

Wales. It was – is – a good book, but its publication coincided with that of the official history, equally good, but longer, more detailed, more ambitious altogether. Several other books on the same subject came out at the same time. A literary editor sent the lot to me, as literary editors will. I was confronted with the reviewer's usual difficulty, whether to devote a paragraph or so to each book, write a general essay or review one book properly and nod politely but perfunctorily towards the rest. I chose the last course and wrote about the official history. I have felt guilty ever since.

Now there is a chance to make amends. Richards's latest book, *Carwyn: A Personal Memoir* (Michael Joseph, £8.95), is equally short but more distinguished. It can be recommended not only to the rugby follower but to anyone interested in Wales. Indeed, it contains very little technical material about the game and the changes which Carwyn James introduced – too little, in my opinion. It is really a long essay on Wales and the Welsh, with Carwyn (as he was always called, without familiarity or affectation) filling the centre of the stage, and the author commentating as chorus.

He comes from Pontypridd in south-east Wales. Carwyn came from Cefneithin in the south-west, in the anthracite coalfield of east Carmarthenshire, as it used to be called before Edward Heath and Peter Walker started messing about with the counties' names. Wales is divided in many respects, notably north and south, east and west, Welsh-speaking and non-Welsh-speaking. Carwyn and the author embodied the last two divisions. Richards resented Carwyn's excluding him from the nation because he could not speak the language – a complaint which other writers, such as Gwyn Thomas, have echoed. (Dylan Thomas, who could not speak Welsh either, did not bother himself with such matters.) The experience of the south-east, Richards used to say, was as valid as, and physically harder than, that of the south-west. This was true enough. Another way of putting it is to say that the east became proletarianised, whereas the west did not. There are several explanations of why this happened.

The east was more popular with immigrants, from across the Bristol Channel, from Scotland (the Kinnocks, for example) and from Ireland (the ancestors of Terry Holmes, presumably). Though Swansea drew some immigrants and to this day maintains a cosmopolitan and somewhat raffish aspect, the drastic changes in population came further east. The Welsh tend to be either self-pitying or boastful, about artistic achievements, for example. They – we – tend to forget real triumphs, among which is the peaceful absorption of Scottish and Irish immigrants, with none of the problems that afflict Liverpool and Glasgow, not to mention Belfast. Then again, the industrial south-west was nearer the countryside. It was this proximity, together with the practice of building detached stone houses (with large gardens) for miners to live in, which bred a set of values and way of life that were partly peasant, partly bourgeois and only partly industrial.

Carwyn's father was a miner who also knew about carpentry, building and farming. The family retained close connections with their original home in Cardiganshire. Carwyn was brought up to speak traditional Welsh. Lapses into the local *patois* were corrected. He was somehow apart, also something of a goody-two-shoes.

He formed an early aversion to the Tammany aspect of Labour politics in south Wales. Later this was transformed into a hostility towards the committeemen of the Welsh Rugby Union. The original cause of this hostility towards the 'fixing' aspects of Welsh life (though it would have been understandable enough in any event) was his failure, as a recent graduate in Welsh of Aberystwyth, to obtain a teaching post at his old grammar school, despite the fact that the headmaster had specifically requested his appointment. County councillors ruled – a typical Welsh complaint. So Carwyn became a Welsh nationalist and, before the journalism and broadcasting of his later years, earned a living teaching at the public school, Llandovery, and at the teachers' training college in Carmarthen.

In the last decade of his life he was, next to Barry John, the most famous living Welshman. He and John had between them defeated New Zealand, the most powerful rugby nation in the world. John also came from Cefneithin and was, like Carwyn, an old boy of the Gwendraeth Valley Grammar

School. They were stopped in the street, their opinions endlessly canvassed. Cefneithin had conquered the world – at any rate the world of rugby. John retired early, perhaps too early, from the game and found some repose in his wife and young family. Carwyn had no such consolation. Indeed, Richards is tactfully reticent about his sexual nature. Girls played little part in his life.

His untidiness was famous, as was his chain-smoking and liking for gin-and-tonic. We met only a few times. The last occasion was in El Vino's, when he appeared at something of a loose end. He would have liked dinner or the theatre with me, but I had to go somewhere else. As usual with these meetings, I wanted to talk to him about rugby; he wanted to talk to me about politics. But I am sorry I did not cancel my arrangements and spend the rest of the evening with him. He seemed lonely, in need of companionship. This was part of his charm – a notoriously difficult quality for a writer to bring out, but Alun Richards succeeds triumphantly.

APPRECIATING IRELAND
The Field, February 1985

Most people who are interested in sport have their favourite teams, who occupy the position they do for no rational reason. Often this has nothing to do with patriotism, national or local. Among national teams, my own favourites include the New Zealanders and the Indians (though not the Pakistanis) in cricket, the Australians and the Irish in rugby. I do have reasons, however. These teams tend not only to be underdogs internationally but to have to compete for sporting recognition within their own countries. Thus Australian rugby has to contend with Rugby League, soccer, Australian rules and, of course, cricket, not to mention tennis and various aquatic pursuits. The Irish selection is not so wide – soccer, hurling and Gaelic football principally.

But rugby in Ireland is played under a particular

disadvantage. It is officially disapproved of by the Irish State, which regards or purports to regard it as somehow insufficiently Celtic. It is all great nonsense. But post-war Irish teams seem to have flourished under it. Rugby is, as far as I know, the only major game in which Irishmen from North and South, Protestant and Catholic, play in the same team. It does not seem to have made the slightest political difference. Sport in this instance has not erected any barriers, as it sometimes does; but neither has it pulled any down. It is a minor miracle that Ireland manages, season after season, to produce teams of the quality it does. This season looks like being a specially good one. I wrote in these pages a few weeks ago that, of the home countries which had at that stage played Australia, Ireland had produced by far the best performance.

Then the Australian manager, Alan Jones, said he thought Ireland would win the championship. Yet at the end of last week the bookmakers were offering 8-1 against Ireland, with France inevitably the favourites, followed by Scotland and then Wales. I do not think these odds reflected any substantial pre-championship weight of money, though I am open to correction by Messrs Ladbroke on this. The odds were presumably the result of the bookies' thinking of a number or, rather, several numbers. If so, they clearly did not know what they were about. Eight to one was a bargain. This remains true irrespective of the final resting place of the championship. Certainly, of the four teams on display on 2 February, Ireland were the outstanding one. Their scrum was as solid as it usually is, though Scotland missed Milne. Their back row were no respecters of persons, though Scotland missed Leslie, as they did Johnston among the backs. Above all, Ireland had Lenihan in the lineout, on this form surely the equal of Norster.

Mick Doyle, the Irish coach, has the distinction of being one of the last flankers to be a normal-looking member of the human race. Indeed he played for the Lions against South Africa weighing only 13 stone and standing five feet ten. He is, however, being a bit of an old silly when he says that he does not intend to 'build the team' round a goal-kicker. No one is asking him to do that. A few may still be asking him to bring back Ward or Campbell, even though Dean did more than enough at Murrayfield to guarantee his place for the rest of the season. (How easily those words trip off the pen! Yet as journalists are as good as their last piece, so half-backs, scrum and stand-off alike, are as good as their last match.) All anyone is asking Doyle to do, really, is give thanks that he has Kiernan in the side, even though he did not kick goals against Scotland as productively as he had against Australia.

If Ireland were the outstanding side, England were the surprising one. I refuse, however, to be force-fed with humble pie. If you think there is any anti-English bias here, I may say that whenever Harlequins met a Welsh club over the past few years, my friends and I agreed that Cooke outclassed the Welsh opposition. He did England proud against France. Even so: the selectors had wisely taken my advice, proffered in a previous column, and brought in Simms, Andrew, Brain and, on the day, an oddly tired-looking Blakeway; others admittedly gave similar advice at greater length. The French won the non-penalty scores 3-1. And they crossed the English line.

I do not, as it happens, blame Estève for vanity or vainglory in trying to ground the ball under or nearer the posts. I do blame him, as he blames himself, for allowing the persistent Harding to knock it out of his hands – a different matter. I wonder what would have happened if the ball had popped out less obviously, and closer to the ground? Referees are now overindulgent about what amounts to grounding the ball, just as they are about forward passes, though they are about little else.

The other interesting aspect to the match was the throwing-in of Gallion. This seemed to work quite well. In an old-fashioned lineout France would have been outplayed even more comprehensively by Orwin and Dooley. It is often forgotten that French wings continued to use the old-style under-arm double-handed scoop throw when other countries had long gone over to the hookers' using the newer overarm one-handed throw. France still won the championship several times.

THE COMMENTARY SITUATION

The Field, March 1985

Many years ago, when France were playing Wales at Cardiff, there was a pile-up, the referee blew his whistle, and the forwards disentangled themselves. A Frenchman was left immobile on the ground. Sponges failed to revive him. Eventually a stretcher was summoned. The horizontal player was borne from the field amid a silence broken only by the solitary voice of a Welsh spectator: 'That's the trouble with them, see. Excitable.'

I did not witness this episode myself. Sir Huw Wheldon assures me it happened. Anyway it makes a nice story. I was reminded of it watching Scotland and France on television. Both the commentator, Nigel Starmer-Smith, and his sidekick, Bill Beaumont, adopted what was to me an insufferably patronising tone about the French. Admittedly they did not play well. They should have beaten Scotland by 20 points or so. The three-quarters – not just poor, shattered Estève – kept fumbling or knocking-on. Lescarboura did not kick well, but Scotland's backs kicked worse. I think Gallion had a good game. The proof of the play is in the possession. For all my colleagues' animadversions on his old-fashioned throwing-in, with the hooker Dintrans at scrum-half, France received much the better ball from the lineout. They deserved to be criticised adversely but not patronised as if they were the second netball team.

I do not wish to be harsh on Beaumont and Starmer-Smith. I have never done their job, do not want to do it and should not be asked to do it even if I desired it. But I have done some commentating on political events such as budgets when they are taking place. And I feel that a gentle protest must be entered on behalf of the television public against the two of them, and also against my compatriot Gareth Edwards from the village of Gwaun-cae-Gurwen.

Bill McLaren, who with Edwards was booked for the England-Wales match that did not take place, is, of course, incomparable. Well, that is not perhaps wholly accurate. He can be compared to Jim Laker and Richie Benaud at cricket,

Peter O'Sullevan at racing. He can come the old Scotch dominie too strongly, perhaps, for some tastes. But at least he knows his stuff. He should, however, stop talking about 'the little man from Llanelli' (formerly Phil Bennett, now Phil Lewis) and about 'the big man from Llanelli' (formerly Delme Thomas or Derek Quinnell) unless he is also prepared to add to his cast a medium-sized man from Llanelli (David Pickering, perhaps?)

I wish I could say the same about his sidekick Gareth Edwards. Edwards's position – and why should he, along with Beaumont, enjoy a quasi-monopolistic position? – seems to me to embody at least two fallacies. The one is that great players can be expected to have something percipient or stimulating to say on all occasions. The other is that Welshmen are fluent and convincing speakers. Very often they are. Gerald Davies and Barry John both are, as Carwyn James was.

But the spoken word is not Edwards's metier. That is not where his genius lies. Not only does he get his syntax in a twist. That does not greatly matter if the speaker has something interesting to say – though it matters more if he is performing without being seen on television, as Edwards usually is, than it does when he is being interviewed or speaking to camera. Edwards, however, uses partly the argot of the soccer manager, 'sheer magic' and the like, partly the mnemonic language of the dumbo coach.

'What did you think of that, Gareth?'

'To me, Bill, it summed up the three Ps: Possession, Pace, Perfection.'

This is just the baby language. He might equally well have added Passing and Position, making it five Ps.

Bill Beaumont, by contrast, has one all-purpose prescription. This is that the team who are losing should 'settle down'. He may add, as he did on Saturday about Scotland, that the forwards should not be afraid to 'take on' the opposition. But his principle seems to be, as it was Lord Stockton's, that cool and calm deliberation disentangles every knot. He has, alas, adopted some of Starmer-Smith's bad linguistic habits, which the latter to his credit seems to be trying to give up, of talking about ruck-situations and maul-situations rather than about rucks and mauls. Why not a scrum-situation or a lineout-situation too?

Starmer-Smith falls into another error. This is to announce with the utmost confidence what a team are going to do seconds before they do it – or, as usually happens, do not do it, but something else entirely. We had an example of this on Saturday. France were pushing the Scottish pack backwards at a rate of knots and they seemed to me to have scored a try. The referee, who was nearer, decided otherwise. 'They'll go for the push over again,' Starmer-Smith proclaimed, or words to this effect. 'No they won't,' I replied. 'As it's their put-in they'll go for a quick heel and use the open side.'

So indeed they did, and nearly scored. What made me crosser, however, was Beaumont's and Starmer-Smith's assumption that all loyal Brits wanted Scotland to win. I want Scotland to win only when they are playing New Zealand or South Africa. I usually want France to win (even over Wales when Wales are playing deliberately dull rugby). On this occasion France did win, just about. But clearly some are *à la lanterne*. I did not like the look of that Fouroux at half time one little bit. His earphones were, I thought, especially sinister. And are they legal in coaches? I think we should be told.

THE WELSH REVELATION
The Field, March 1985

The interesting way in which the championship is turning out is not as surprising as all that. It is a tribute to us armchair critics. England brought in Rob Andrew, Kevin Simms and Paul Dodge and drew with France. Wales brought back Gareth Davies and beat Scotland. Ireland did not take our advice in that they omitted to bring back Ollie Campbell or Tony Ward. But in Michael Kiernan they luckily had a kicker who did everything Ward or Campbell could have done – as he had shown he could do earlier in the Australian match. In any case we armchair critics were at one with the Australian manager Alan Jones, and opposed (or were grateful to) the bookmakers in thinking that Ireland had a good chance of the championship; as they still have, though I do not fancy them to win at Cardiff.

I cannot resist quoting the Irish coach Mick Doyle on France before the match on 2 March: 'They're a very enigmatic outfit. They can mix the brilliant with the unexpected.' I hope that in reporting this I do not get into trouble with the department of the People's Republic of Islington (where I live) which is dedicated to extirpating the Irish joke. In fact the match turned out to be what is called a 'bruising encounter', though some of the injuries were clearly nastier.

The revelation was of course Wales. Why 'of course'? It is a treacherous, eliding little phrase which writers tend to insert to give an air of spurious smoothness to their prose. Here it is justified. The history is as follows. A few years ago the Welsh selectors – sometimes viewed in the Principality as deacons of the chapel but more often as bedraggled remnants of Fred Karno's army – reshaped the side. They did so mainly through necessity but partly through choice. At first things seemed to be going reasonably well. Then there were setbacks. And there was a disaster at Cardiff, when Scotland ran round Wales and loyal voters had to turn the television off in the second half, so painful had the spectacle become to them. The more recent Australian match was not as shocking to national self-esteem as this, but it was nonetheless humiliating.

Win or lose, however, up or down, there were two great questions. Who was to be the stand-off half, Gareth Davies or Malcolm Dacey? And what was to be done about the back row? The former question the selectors answered – not initially, but the second time round – by preferring Dacey against the weight of rugby opinion. For once this opinion favoured the Cardiff player and college boy. The east-west and college-non-college division or cross-division (for non-college boys can come from the east too, just as college boys can come from the west) is fundamental to an understanding of Welsh rugby controversies and the bitterness they engender: a bitterness which led to the retirement from international rugby of the much-attacked Welsh No 8 and Cambridge Blue, Eddie Butler, on the eve of the announcement of the team for the Scottish match.

It is tempting to explain this perpetual Welsh dispute as a reflection of similar cross-country arguments, to do with relative prosperity and 'favouritism'. There is, however, some rugby history to it as well. During the inter-war period and, indeed, for some time after the last war the Welsh rugby team was run by Captain Walter Rees from his home in Neath. 'Captain' Rees had been awarded this rank as a recruiting officer during the First World War and insisted on it, though he had never been a regular soldier. (Even then it would, I believe, have been solecistic to use it.) Captain Rees was a stickler for correct expenses or, rather, he was mean about them – insisting that players could have walked instead of taking the bus, deducting sums for meals they would have had to buy for themselves anyway, that kind of thing. At the same time he had a tremendous weakness for Blues, though he was not himself an alumnus of one of our ancient universities. In his eyes a Blue could do little wrong, even with his expenses.

Some of Walter Rees's young men did Wales proud in the somewhat barren period between the two wars, notably Windsor Lewis, Cliff Jones and Wilfred Wooller. Others, usually with hyphenated Welsh names, were less successful. But the popular or populist case against the college boys was not so much that they were no good as that they kept the great Llanelli centre Albert Jenkins out of the side. Albert, though of a simple and affectionate disposition, could scarcely write his own name.

Gareth Davies was not in Albert's position, even though, as an old pupil of the Gwendraeth Valley Grammar School, he was – is – regarded as an honorary Llanelli player. But Eddie Butler was no doubt unfairly seen as one of those Rees-Jones figures from the past, keeping some humbler citizen out of the side. Yet whom was he keeping out? There was no obviously commanding figure. The selectors switched

Richard Moriarty from blind-side flanker to No 8, brought in the hitherto largely unregarded policeman Martyn Morris in his place and retained David Pickering. Pickering had the match of a lifetime – I wonder whether it will be remembered as Pickering's match, as Paxton's or as the French referee's? Mark Ring had the same kind of game as Pickering, though he was both luckier and unluckier. Moriarty, who reminds me of a dray horse with a nasty temper, disported himself with agility. Morris did well.

But Pickering apart – a man who should be encouraged because he is of a normal size – I am still unconvinced that the back row is right, that Jeff Whitefoot is a fair exchange for Ian Stephens, that Phil Lewis is a better wing than Adrian Hadley (or an international wing at all) and that Billy James is a more accomplished hooker than M. Richards. Still, though those who put money on Ireland made a good investment, Wales are now the only side that can win the Grand Slam – if they can keep clear of French referees.

ENGLAND'S BAFFLING CHOICE OF BACKS
The Field, March 1985

The late Iain Macleod never missed a Calcutta Cup match. Or so he liked to claim. I suspect that in sport, as in politics, Iain was something of an old Scottish romantic whose practice differed from his preaching. I confess that as an occasion it has not held much allure for me. It is rather a hipflask kind of game. I have never myself been able to see the charm of swigging neat whisky on a cold afternoon from a receptacle at which several other citizens have had a go. I would rather have a cup of hot Bovril any day.

Ten years ago I saw Hancock's Try. Andy Hancock of Northampton, who was like an inverted equilateral triangle (I was always surprised that he weighed only 12 stone), ran down the left touchline to draw the match for England three-all. My friend Frank Keating of *The Guardian*, in his preliminary piece before the match of 16 March, got Hancock's weight and build right but remembered him running very fast. He was no slowcoach, though he was no Ken Jones or J. J. Williams either, but I remember his try taking an age, as if he were pedalling a bicycle through wet sand. He seemed most anxious to be rid of the ball, looking over this shoulder, turning this way and that. But, as no Englishman seemed conveniently to hand, on he ploughed.

In this respect most modern players, presented with an opportunity of a long run following an interception, a dropped pass, a miskick or whatever, tend to adopt Hancock's self-effacing technique – though unlike him they usually fail to score. They change direction, look round, appear agitated; the more so if they are backs. Forwards such as Iain Paxton appear to be bolder spirits. When Jeremy Hughes of London Welsh, in the recent quarter-final of the John Player Cup, intercepted a pass virtually on his own line and ran the length of the field to score against Waterloo without once looking back, why, it was an exceptional incident.

England and Scotland produced no comparable score this time. It is fair to say that England should have won convincingly in the first half, Scotland in the second. A draw would have been a fairer result, I think. Poor old Scotland are now out of things. England are in a position to win the Triple Crown and the championship, though I shall be surprised if they win either. There are, however, several faults – or rather wrong selections – among the English backs which are remediable. Chris Martin came into the line too slowly. I do not see what Nick Stringer has done wrong to exclude him from further consideration – or why the selectors are not bold enough, alternatively, to try out Stuart Barnes in what is probably his natural position. Barnes looks like becoming one of those players who fail to realise their talents because they play out of position.

There are no clear rules or binding precedents in this area. Long ago it was thought, for instance, that the great Bleddyn Williams was a natural stand-off half rather than a centre. He played one unhappy international in that position against England and promptly reverted to the centre. Yet the almost equally great Mike Gibson made the reverse change, from stand-off to centre, with complete success. David Duckham's move from centre to wing was equally happy, as was Gerald Davies's. On the other hand, there have been fine players such as Derek Quinnell, Roger Uttley and Peter Morgan who have never settled – or been allowed to settle down.

A head of steam has been building up in the Press for the return of Barnes at stand-off in place of Rob Andrew. Aberrant place-kicker though he may be, I hope Andrew is given the further chance which he had already earned. Richard Harding's service in the Scottish match was slow and ballooning. In addition the English scrum, admirable in most other respects, tended to play silly, pointless games in releasing or, rather, not releasing the ball. The selectors have bowed to the demand for the return of the unlucky (a Calvinist would say doomed or damned) Nigel Melville to partner Barnes. This is all very well. But again I ask what has the worthy Richard Hill done wrong to exclude him from further consideration? Truly the English selectors move in mysterious ways.

One of the mysteries concerns Paul Dodge: not only his captaincy but his record of 28 caps, equalling Jeff Butterfield's and also, indeed, what now seems to be his unchallengeable place in the side. My Press colleagues write sapiently that he is a steadying influence, a players' player. I do not want to be unkind, but I am reminded of the barrister who could hardly string two consecutive sentences together but who continued to be given briefs. 'He may not be much of an advocate,' solicitors and colleagues at the bar would nod to one another, 'but, by God, he knows his law.'

A PERSONAL SELECTION
The Field, April 1985

Before I come to the players' records, I should like to write a few words about my own. I overestimated France and Wales, underestimated England – though their match with Wales has still to be played – and got Scotland and Ireland about right. I certainly agree that the Scots were unlucky; just as I do that the Irish were lucky. At least I correctly predicted the champions. The other toasts, in no particular order, are to the Australian Alan Jones, who first said the Irish would win; Mick Doyle, who coached them; Ciaran Fitzgerald, who captained them; Michael Kiernan, who kicked their goals; and Messrs Ladbroke and others, who offered the ludicrously generous odds of 8-1 against them.

Let us now pretend to be British Isles or Barbarian selectors and try to pick the best 15 of ... I was about to write 'of those players seen during the season'. But this is to limit ourselves unnecessarily; unjustly also as far as individuals are concerned. In the full-back position alone, numerous semi-retired, discarded or injured players compare favourably with those who have held down the job for their country during the season. Among those rejected for one reason or another, including self-rejection, are Andy Irvine, Dusty Hare, Nick Stringer, Howell Davies and Gwyn Evans. Still, I should play safe and have Peter Dods as first choice. My second choice would be Paul Thorburn, whom, I may say, I should have nominated on the strength of his performances for Neath even if he had not won a first cap against France.

The wings virtually choose themselves: Simon Smith and Rory Underwood, both of England. As recently as the end of last season Mark Titley, Adrian Hadley and John Carleton (whom Smith dislodged, justifiably as it turned out, though Carleton had never let England down) would all have been in contention. No longer. My reserves would be the old reliable Trevor Ringland, accompanied by his Irish team-mate Keith Crossan rather than by Roger Baird.

The centres present greater difficulties. They usually do. I should not like either to tackle or to be tackled by Robert Ackerman, who increasingly resembles an East German female shot-putter; but his lack of pace is becoming more apparent.

Mark Ring, by contrast, is probably the discovery of the season among the backs of all the home countries. There is a campaign in the Principality to choose him along with the almost equally elusive Bleddyn Bowen, who was originally Ackerman's Welsh partner. In the Lions I should settle for Ring and Kiernan, with Bowen and the gangling but gifted Brendan Mullin as reserves.

But who would have thought that Ollie Campbell, Tony Ward equally, would have been forgotten so quickly? Yet so it is. Paul Dean is now established. In the English match he outpunted Rob Andrew. Several critics would now make him second, even first choice. I should prefer to stick to Gareth Davies, who, having dealt with Malcolm Dacey's usurpation, now has another rival in Jonathan Davies of Neath: the stand-off half scene in Wales is as *mouvementé* as the property market in Islington.

My scrum-halves are I fear equally unadventurous. Terry Holmes had an up-and-down season with an 'up' against France. When he started his career, Welshmen said: 'He's going to be even better than Gareth Edwards.' Now they say: 'He was never as good as Gareth when you come down to it.' This is sad. This is life. But it is not to depreciate Holmes, who has not had the best of luck with injuries, any more than poor Nigel Melville has. My second choice would be an old war horse, Roy Laidlaw, rather than Melville.

Colin Deans remains the outstanding hooker. As his reserve I should have Alan Phillips of Cardiff, unjustly passed over by the Welsh selectors. The first choice tight-head is fairly easy: Iain Milne. On the loose-head I should have Ian Stephens of Bridgend, a Welsh reserve for most of the season. Phil Blakeway could be the reserve on either side of the hooker; I am not sure about the fourth prop.

Nor am I certain who the fourth lock ought to be: Robert Norster and Donal Lenihan as first choices, certainly, followed by Willie Anderson. But then who? Not John Perkins, I trust. He is generally worth at least six points to the other side in the penalties he gives them.

Talent in the back row is by contrast abundant – except in Wales. England could assemble two back rows both of Lions standard. Yet Iain Paxton has to be in at No 8 because of his performance in the Welsh match. He is heavily challenged by Brian Spillane. David Pickering must be in for the same reason as Paxton, and also because of his performance in the French match. His challengers are more numerous: David Cooke, Gary Rees, and Peter Winterbottom (all of England), David Leslie and Nigel Carr. I should settle for John Hall of England on the other side, challenged by Philip Matthews of Ireland and several Scotsmen, including the unjustly dropped Jim Calder.

The final team is: Dods; Smith, Ring, Kiernan, Underwood; Davies, Holmes; Milne, Deans, Stephens, Lenihan, Norster, Hall, Paxton, Pickering. The sad moral is that not much new talent has emerged since the Lions tour of New Zealand. My own selection would I am afraid meet the same fate as the Lions. They would probably go down to the French too. We should perhaps do better to choose the entire Irish team instead.

TWICKENHAM RITUALS
The Field, May 1985

On Cup final day we met at The Sun in Richmond: John Edwards of the *Daily Mail* with Mrs Edwards, Grenville Jones, Tim Wilton the actor, John Coker of the BBC, formerly of Oxford University and Harlequins, and my son, from the Cranfield Institute of Technology. A mixed bag, you might say, though with a distinct bias towards what Tony Benn calls The Meejer. This is where we usually meet before the match when London Welsh are at home. Rugby pubs, like rugby clubs, go in and out of fashion. We used to meet in a Richmond wine bar, but for some reason which I forget this failed to continue giving satisfaction.

Afterwards – on normal Saturdays, I mean, not this particular one – we stand on the duck boards behind the goalposts at Old Deer Park. We do this even in the most inclement weather, when Coker produces a golf umbrella. On these occasions, when the weather is bad, I may retire to the Press seats in the stand, to accusations of softness, grandeur or both. This is part of the ritual; as is Grenville Jones's estimate of the size of the Old Deer Park crowd. 'Four thousand, would you say?' Jones says, when there are clearly no more than 1,500 there, if that. When the play is down at the other end of the field, and nothing much seems to be going on, we can have quite lengthy and animated discussions about the numbers present.

At a quarter to two The Sun was out of anything to eat. I said that in Toulouse, where I had lately been on holiday, the bar and café management would have anticipated the event, laying in great stocks of *baguettes, jambon, fromages, saucisses, saucissons, rillettes* and what-have-you. Alternatively, they would have sent out for supplies and resold them at modest profit to the hungry rugby enthusiasts of south-western France. My friends looked at me sadly, as if too much southern sun or wine or something had gone to my head. This was Cup final day, was it not? And on such days pubs were expected to run out of food. It was part of the fun, like having one's ribs crushed, or exchanging pleasantries with the constabulary. ('That's no way to speak to a person in authority,' I heard a policeman say to a Bath supporter at Twickenham station.)

The absence of food was made tolerable by my knowledge of the small supermarket, now run by Asians, between Twickenham station and the ground. It is on the left, part of a stretch of three or four shops, just before you arrive on foot at the big roundabout on the Chertsey Road. It sells (besides beer) excellent meat and vegetable samosas. Nor had it run out of them on this Saturday.

The singing in The Sun had not been up to much really. But it had been raucous enough for one neutral rugby follower to say: 'If this is going to be decided by supporters the Welsh have got it sewn up already.' This proved a sadly incorrect prediction, not only of the course and result of the game, but also of the level of support. The Bath supporters seemed to me younger, fitter, noisier and more numerous.

We Welshmen, predominantly teachers, I fancy, were out with our families: not just, as I was, with a large son of 25 who could look after himself but, more often, with small children and sometimes wives as well. The Bath supporters, by contrast, were preponderantly male, in their teens or early 20s, tending to move in groups of between six and 12. They were more like soccer supporters. Please do not misunderstand me. I am making no accusations whatever of violence or misbehaviour; merely pointing out that the Bath supporters were different. Perhaps this was inevitable. The West Country was coming to town. West Country supporters, of the Bristol soccer teams or the Somerset, though not so much the Gloucester, cricket team, tend to – shall we say? – exuberance. And cup competitions in most games attract noisier supporters anyway.

Neil Kinnock was at one and the same time the traditional and the more modern kind of Welsh supporter. He was attending both with his son, which is traditional, and with his wife, which is more modern. Some of his parliamentary entourage were with him too. We came upon them quite by chance. They were sitting not with the rugby nobs but in the upper west stand. Kinnock had been asked to sit with the toffs but had not wanted to accept the hospitality of the tobacco firm involved. This puzzled me slightly because he does after all smoke a pipe – and there is nothing, as far as I know, especially iniquitous about Imperial Tobacco. I was also told he simply wished to be with his friends. It was not clear precisely which; perhaps a bit of both. There is no conflict or contradiction. Anyway I thought it was to the credit of Kinnock, sitting there with his family in his red and white scarf, having presumably paid for his seat. Afterwards he led the singing in the Surrey Bowls Club at Old Deer Park. It was better in defeat than it had been in The Sun beforehand. Very Welsh, that.

LEADING LIGHTS OF LEICESTER
The Field, September 1985

Statistics have never been a part of rugby as they are of cricket, which is probably a blessing (though sometimes I could do with a few more of them). But by most tests Leicester are the outstanding English club side of the last decade. They have reached the final of the John Player Cup five times in this period and won it three times. They cause apprehension in the best clubs throughout Britain.

Their former coach, H. V. 'Chalkie' White (the pet name has the thudding inevitability of most such appellations in England, though 'Dusty' Hare is slightly more original), was the second-best coach in these islands during that time. Hare was the second-best British full-back. He was undoubtedly the best in England, even if the English selectors behaved as they usually do when they have available to them a really outstanding player. This they see as a marvellous opportunity to drop him and restore him to the side as often as they can, just for the hell of it. There have been, and still are, two equally fine performers in Peter Wheeler and Rory Underwood.

Underwood, with his south-east Asian face and prop-forward thighs, has the gift which all great sportsmen possess, that of communicating excitement. Whenever he gets the ball, as he does quite often for Leicester, less often for England, and hardly at all for the Royal Air Force, there is a whiff of danger, of fire and brimstone in the air.

The service authorities seem to be behaving rather selfishly over Underwood, who is training to be a pilot and always appears to be off on some course or other. This is not, I may add, a question of forcing him to give priority to the RAF side over club or county. If you choose to join the armed forces it seems to me fair enough that you should be required to turn out for their team, at any rate in the inter-services championship, joke though that competition now is.

But Underwood's 'courses' seem to go on and on. Hardly has he finished one when he is starting another, lost to the rugby field for months rather than weeks. Training to be a pilot is a difficult and demanding business, no doubt. But training for other occupations can be equally, if not more, arduous and exacting. Such training does not require the subject to be sequestered as if in a monastery. If Underwood were in the Romanian air force we may be sure that the party comrades would have him disporting himself on the field virtually daily.

I have never been able to understand the indulgence which several respected rugby writers, notably my friend Clem Thomas, display towards the Romanian national side. Most of them appear to be officers in the Romanian army. This is a question not of communism but of professionalism. They are being paid to play rugby. That the Olympic authorities have passed by on the other side when confronted by Iron Curtain (and not only Iron Curtain) bogus amateurism is no reason for the rugby authorities to do likewise.

Which is a convenient point to pass to Peter Wheeler, for he was said to have been involved in the 'boot money scandal'. Another description of him is the unofficial 'shop steward' of the English side. He was certainly passed over for the England captaincy when he was the natural candidate. His omission from the Lions side that went recently to New Zealand was simpler to explain but harder to justify. The captain was Ciaran Fitzgerald because the (managerially) disastrous W.J. McBride insisted on it, and the reserve was Colin Deans, whereas the two hookers should have been Deans and Wheeler. The latter is entitled to feel aggrieved. But he is a cheerful soul who has, in addition, written a good autobiography.

About Paul Dodge I am more ambivalent; as a player, I mean. There is no doubt that he is well spoken of, by other players and by experienced commentators alike. He is said to be a steadying influence, doing good by stealth. Some would describe him as a players' player; I should be more inclined to describe him as a commentators' favourite. He is strong and he can kick. But – I may have been unlucky – I have never seen him do anything interesting or exciting. Just so, the wise men reply. It is not Dodge's function to be interesting or exciting. That is not his historic role. His role is certainly not to speak for England on television. Last year, as captain, he was to English rugby what Leon Brittan was to the Conservative government. He had problems as a communicator – even though he may have been better looking than Brittan, which is not difficult.

The more obviously talented Clive Woodward has been disappointing for England, rather as the similar player David Richards has been for Wales. Les Cusworth has been unlucky with the selectors while Nick Youngs has been luckier.

The Leicester supporters are enthusiastic but well behaved. In their red, green and white rugby shirts, their matching scarves, club ties, and green pullovers, they clearly spend a lot of money on their supporters' garb. This is only right, coming as they do from the knitwear capital of England.

CROSS PURPOSES BETWEEN CLUBS
The Field, October 1985

Just as the political year begins, as far as I am concerned, with the Labour conference, so does the rugby year with the match between Harlequins and Llanelli. For as long as I can remember this has been a Quins home fixture; but sometimes, when there are early season representative matches of one kind or another at the Rugby Union headquarters, it is played at the Stoop Memorial ground. There are some people who are fond of Stoop, because it is more like an ordinary club ground than Twickenham is. For social purposes the Quins players retire to the Stoop clubroom after they have spent an hour or so mixing with the nobs in the bar at HQ.

I prefer the big ground at Twickenham, which has the charm of a splendid seaside resort that is perpetually out of season. 'You ought to see the lavatories at Twickenham,' my father used to say to me. 'As big as houses.' He was accustomed to the squalid facilities then offered by the St Helen's ground, Swansea, or the Arms Park, Cardiff – I will not go into the disgusting details. It was easy, later, to see what he had meant. Most Welshmen are, however, ambivalent about the place, both fascinated and repelled by it, accommodating as it does as many ghosts as the Arms Park, and more menacing ghosts at that.

51

But usually Llanelli and Quins is quite a jolly occasion, as club matches played at Twickenham go. In most seasons it is not just the only Anglo-Welsh game in London on that Saturday but also the only game worth seeing at all. It was not so this September. London Welsh had decided to play Leicester on the same day. A lot of people (by no means all of them London Welshmen) who have normally gone to Twickenham to see Llanelli trotted off instead to Old Deer Park to see Leicester.

In *The Field*'s sister, or maybe cousin, publication, the *Daily Mail*, the journalists have a phrase, 'why oh why', as in: 'Let's have a why-oh-why piece' on whatever it happens to be – miners' ballots, Conservative chairmen or the like. Similarly I ask: why oh why did London Welsh have to arrange a fixture with Leicester? Richmond used to be the principal culprits in this regard, though later on in the season, arranging attractive home games with Swansea, Neath and Llanelli on Saturdays when there were equally if not more attractive games on in London.

The Llanelli fixture with Richmond was, it may be remembered, cancelled six years ago, after Chris Ralston had been 'raked' by R. Powell. Powell was – is – an Englishman who also played for Gloucester and, indeed, had an England trial. Ralston's father was, understandably, angry about the violence done to his son on this occasion and, less understandably, started to mutter about legal action against the culprit or culprits. Unsurprisingly, the then Llanelli team took alarm, and decided to clam up completely. As a Llanelli official said to me at the time: 'They're simple boys, and this talk of courts and the law frightened them.' One does not have to be simple to be frightened by threats of legal action: indeed, alarm is a sign of sense. But Ralston senior did not pursue the cause, and on 21 September Powell was Llanelli's linesman at Twickenham.

It was not just his presence there then that makes me recall this old (and, briefly, notorious) incident. It is instructive to remember it also because it is relevant to the early preoccupations of this season: violence in general, violence during Anglo-Welsh encounters in particular, and the value, or not, of these matches to English or Welsh rugby. I hope it is not an indication of chauvinism on my part when I say that the visits of Welsh clubs in England are looked forward to more eagerly than the visits of English clubs in Wales. England is more admiring, or hospitable. Welsh clubs usually increase the gate. A full, exclusive league system would fail in England, as it does not fail in more conservative Scotland, because of the Anglo-Welsh fixtures. Some English clubs say modestly that these fixtures help them to maintain, even to increase their standards. To which one obvious question is: why, then, is the Welsh national team not more impressive than it now is? Of that, more in another column.

These fixtures also have a reputation for violence. My own impression is that violent play is more common in 'derby' matches, whether between two Welsh sides or two English. Thus Newport and Bristol is simultaneously an Anglo-Welsh battle and a western derby. It does not, however, have a specially bad reputation.

A lot of typewriter ribbons have been worn away on the affair of George Crawford. Many observers have written that Crawford was right and wrong at the same time: right to want to do something about violence, wrong to walk off, but a fine fellow nonetheless, God bless him, and more power to his elbow. The world of rugby is oversentimental sometimes.

The Quins game was no classic but it was enjoyable. And it showed us a Welsh wing of the future in Ieuan Evans – even though at Twickenham he was at full-back. The announcer had difficulty pronouncing his Christian name: Ee-Eye-Ann.

FALL AND RISE OF THE CENTRE
The Field, October 1985

Though this column is supposed to be about rugby, I should like to begin with a conversation about cricket which I had a few years ago with Michael Brotherton, then Conservative Member for Louth. We were chatting in Annie's Bar, and I ventured to describe Tom Graveney as a great batsman. The florid legislator, who knew a lot about cricket, looked affronted. Great, he said, was a big word, not one to be employed lightly. Compton, he continued, was a great batsman, as were Hutton, May, the Richardses (Barry and Vivian), Harvey and Pollock. Graveney was a very good batsman.

In rugby great players are produced more often in some position than in others. The last couple of decades, for instance, have seen several great stand-off halves – David Watkins, Barry John, Phil Bennett, Hugo Porta and Tony Ward, even though the Irish selectors did not appear to agree with me about Ward. In the same period great centres have been harder to come by. I can think of only one, Mike Gibson, and he began his career as a stand-off. It is sad that the most capped Welsh centre not only in this period but in the entire history of Welsh rugby was Steve Fenwick, with 30.

Part of the explanation lies in the general deterioration in British back play which occurred in the 1970s. Coaches started to look for one 'banger' who would tackle hard, preferably 'turning' his opponent, when the other side had the ball and would crash into his opponent, setting up 'second phase possession', when he himself had the ball. The logic of this would have been inside and outside centres with the banger inside. This did not happen. Clubs and home counties continued mostly with the traditional pattern of left and right centres. The natural, even inevitable development was that instead of one banger coaches began to choose two.

The same period saw centres enjoying, if that is the word, butterfly lives; here one season, gone the next. Did they disappear because of the new pattern of play? Or was the tendency present anyway? It seems that great centres in the traditional mould are individualistic characters. They do not like being told how to play. They do not care much for training either. They were rather like Sir Alf Ramsey's wingers. They were simply forced out of the game, no place for them in it.

An early example was Ken Jones of Llanelli, Oxford University, Cardiff and Wales. He won 14 caps, true. But he

54

had been heralded as a schoolboy as the finest Welsh centre since Bleddyn Williams. He never quite attained the latter's standard. He always seemed to be dispirited by having too much asked of him, and slightly bored. Roy Bergiers of Llanelli came and went. Peter Morgan, still playing for and this season captaining the same club, was never given the chance to settle properly into the Welsh side, though he is only 26 now.

Slightly earlier, Gerald Davies had moved from centre to wing, and possessed both the talent and the strength of character to enforce the change on various panels of selectors. An almost equally great player, David Duckham, made the same decision. In both cases we gained a wing but lost a centre. Meanwhile David Richards and Clive Woodward – both scorers of memorable, but for them scarce, international tries as centres – were somehow failing to come off. Woodward has now emigrated to Australia; Richards stays in Swansea. The most consistent exponents of traditional centre play were the Scots, with Keith Robertson, Jim Renwick and David Johnston. But Johnston was often injured, Renwick was getting on in years, while the Scottish selectors could never make up their minds whether Robertson was a centre or a wing.

This season, however, there are signs of change. If we have no great centres, players with the more traditional skills are gaining greater favour. I do not mean to suggest, by the way, that swerving, jinking and sidestepping are the beginning and end of centre play. Jo Maso of Narbonne was undoubtedly a great centre, and the beauty of his play resided largely in his perfection in giving and taking a pass.

We have no one as good as Maso. But the landscape is not wholly bleak. The English selectors have, I see, come round to agreeing with me about the dullness of Paul Dodge, though I still feel sorry for him. But why no place in the squad for John Palmer of Bath? It is a scandal that he has only two caps, both against South Africa last year. He is fast, strong and elusive, and he can kick. He is certainly the most convincing English centre I have seen this year. Instead a place goes to his Bath colleague Simon Halliday.

Now I have nothing against Halliday. But for years, ever since he left Oxford, he has been marked down by journalists and selectors alike as a future England player. Only a nasty injury, from which he has courageously recovered, prevented him from being capped several years ago. He is in short a selectors' favourite, what the Welsh call a college boy, which does not mean simply that he went to Oxford College, but also that he is unjustly preferred because he went there. One could say the same of Kevin Simms, Fran Clough, Rob Andrew and Stuart Barnes. Indeed the only college boy who seems to have received less than his deserts is Huw Davies. It will be interesting to see how he prospers as a full-back. I should pick him like a shot.

But I do not want to end on a carping note. England have the players already mentioned plus Jamie Salmon. Wales have Kevin Hopkins, Mark Ring and Bleddyn Bowen, if only any two of them can be produced fit and well on a given afternoon. Ireland have Brendan Mullin and Michael Kiernan. Centres are back in fashion – I hope.

ENGLISH OPTIONS
The Field, November 1985

The most entertaining match I have seen so far this season was between Harlequins and Gloucester at Twickenham, when the home side scored more than 40 points to a converted penalty try. As Preedy, Mills, Orwin and Gadd were all playing – none too enthusiastically at times – I did not come away reposing any great hopes in England's future in the international championship. To be fair, Gloucester's defeat was not their forwards' fault; while, to be logical, Quins had David Cooke, Chris Butcher, Olver, Curtis, Salmon and Rose, all England possibles, playing on their side. So one might equally well be encouraged by their victory.

Is Marcus Rose a possible England full-back this season? I do not see why not. He was pitched into the side four years ago, when Dusty Hare was still clearly the best full-back in England, maybe in the British Isles. Hare was justly restored. Nevertheless the selectors did not extend the same toleration to Rose as they did last season to Chris Martin. On balance both he and Rose are out of contention, which I think a pity as far as the latter is concerned.

We now have the embarrassing situation where the two leading candidates, Huw Davies and Nick Stringer, play for the same club, Wasps. That loyalty to clubs which is such a feature of rugby in the south-east is admirable in its way: but this is ridiculous. One of them should take himself off to Saracens, Blackheath, Richmond or Rosslyn Park.

The wings will cause the selectors few worries. Simon Smith and Rory Underwood are the best pair in the championship, while Underwood is possibly the best left-wing in the world. Is he also the fastest? Another wing was in no doubt: 'No, Estève is faster.' 'With or without the ball?' a third party interjected, referring to the French three-quarter's Twickenham disaster at Richard Harding's hands.

Centres are more worrying. For more than a year I have been banging on about the inadequacies of Paul Dodge but take no pleasure in his rather brutal demotion. For reasons that I went into two weeks ago, I think Kevin Simms, Fran Clough and Simon Halliday are being overpromoted. I should settle for John Palmer and Jamie Salmon.

With the half-backs it is a question not only of the best players but of the best pairing. The English selectors have never seemed to see this. In the old days, when England played Wales in January (as they are doing this season, as it happens), there was the joke that the English scrum-half was always dropped, and not just dropped, but never seen or heard of again, sucked into some terrible black hole under the Twickenham west stand. There seem to me to be three interesting pairings from five players: Stuart Barnes and Nigel Melville, Barnes and Hill or Rob Andrew and Richard Moon. I should settle for the first, while the last is the most potentially exciting.

There are some good hookers about: Steve Brain, Andy Simpson and John Olver. The selectors will rightly persevere with Brain, I should think.

The props, by contrast, are a bit of a mess. Some of my colleagues in the writing trade, who have never been in a scrum in their lives, are what I call Front Row Fetishists. They talk to a few gnarled old lags after the match and think they know what went on. They also, in their writing, encourage illegal play. So far this season front row play has not been especially dirty, but the new laws do not seem to have had much effect on packing. I should not pick Gareth Chilcott both because he does not look like a member of the human race and, more important, because he concedes penalties by his very presence on the field: he is referee-prone, as Paul Ringer used to be. I should settle for Gary Pearce and Malcolm Preedy, which is not very exciting, I agree, but what else can one do?

The locks are almost as difficult. Wade Dooley was one of the successes of last season, and John Orwin came on well. But the wandering boy Maurice Colclough has now settled in Swansea, for the time being. In his Angoulême days a friend of mine asked him what his business was, to which he replied: 'Importation and exportation.' The intrepid entrepreneur was almost back to his best form when I saw him playing for Swansea against Harlequins. 'That surely isn't Colclough, is it?' 'Can't be, must be Richard Moriarty, he's put on weight.' But Colclough it was. I should restore the old firm of him and Steve Bainbridge.

England have an abundance but an imbalance of talent in the back row, with three fine open-side flankers in David Cooke, Gary Rees and the still injured Peter Winterbottom, one excellent blind-side specialist in Jon Hall and an awkward gap at No 8. Wales had a similar though not exactly parallel problem, which they solved by playing two open-siders, David Pickering and Gareth Roberts. England could do likewise, with Rees and Cooke as flankers, and Hall at No 8. Dean Richards of Leicester must be a possibility too. I should bring back Paul Simpson if he is still available – he is not now in the Bath side – though at No 6 rather than 8. A forward cannot be a hero against New Zealand, as Simpson was two years ago, yet useless thereafter.

My team would be: H. Davies; S. Smith, J. Palmer, J.

Salmon, R. Underwood; S. Barnes, N. Melville; G. Pearce, S. Brain, M. Preedy, M. Colclough, S. Bainbridge, P. Simpson, J. Hall, D. Cooke (captain).

POOR OLD LONDON WELSH
The Field, November 1985

It was quite like old times two weeks ago at Old Deer Park. The sun shone, the stand was overflowing, the other spectators stood six or more deep on the touchline and Nigel Starmer-Smith was in the commentary box (though it is more a hut on stilts) for *Rugby Special*. The Fijians were making their solitary visit to London – indeed to England. About 8,000 voters had turned out to see them.

Rather more than a decade ago Llanelli or even Harlequins would have attracted six or seven thousand, Cardiff eight or nine. What people usually say is that London Welsh are not the team they used to be in the days of John Dawes and the rest. This is true enough, though I think Colyn Price and Mark Douglas are more skilful half-backs, Tim Jones, Byron Light and Bruce Bradley a stronger front row, than their equivalents in the great era. Romanticising the past is perhaps inevitable if you have any sense of history – a sense which totalitarian governments try to destroy. But we do not have to say that everything was better. This applies to half-backs and front rows too.

Ten to 15 years ago rugby crowds generally were bigger than they are today. Recently I was sitting next to John Coker, formerly of Oxford University and Harlequins, in the Twickenham stand, watching Cardiff in the company of a few thousand other souls. Coker said that in his day they would have had about 10,000 there for Cardiff.

In 1946 my father took me to see Llanelli and Swansea at Stradey Park. There were 20,000 there. The immediate post-war period was the time for big crowds, in soccer and cricket as much as in rugby. So the smaller crowds at Old Deer Park cannot be blamed exclusively on the home team.

But the poor old London Welsh have been having a rather sad time so far this season. What makes it worse is that it is their centenary season, with a centenary history by Stephen Jones and numerous centenary matches of a more or less glamorous character, some already played, others yet to come. Perhaps the moral is that one should not advertise anniversaries. The wisdom in the Surrey Bowls Club, where the true *aficionados* repair for a glass of refreshment after the match rather than to the main clubhouse, is that the overseas tour undertaken before the start of the season was a great mistake. It was, it appears, arranged for the players' benefit, not that of the club. They wanted to 'enjoy themselves, see, have a free holiday, like'. They were tired out before the season began.

I cannot see why players of an amateur game should not enjoy themselves if they are given the chance. Anyway the theory, or diagnosis, is not wholly convincing. In mid-September the Welsh, missing their then first-choice full-back, Matthew Ebsworth, together with their two first-choice centres, Dan Fouhy and Robert Ackerman, put up an excellent display against a Barbarians side of Lions strength. Since then Ackerman has returned – though he is now leaving for Cardiff to better himself – while Fouhy has been out with an injury for the whole season. Ebsworth, who used to play stand-off half for Northampton, has been relegated in favour of Andy Martin, who used to play wing for Cambridge University. Yet only Llanelli have been beaten – gloriously, by one point.

I am tempted to suggest that Clive Rees, the captain, should drop himself. But two weeks ago he saved one Fijian try with a fine tackle from behind or behind-and-across. Tackling from the front has never been Rees's forte: he tends to run between the man with the ball and the man inside or outside him. However, if he saved one try, he missed scoring himself in the first quarter where a younger wing, such as Andrew Yeandle, might have scored. Still, it would be too cruel. He remains one of those players who give a sense of occasion by their mere presence. It is not just that he is liable to do something exciting, which is becoming increasingly rare with him, but also that he is likely to do something funny, even plain silly, anyway something to make us laugh. Crowds' favourites are not always identical with those of commentators or selectors. But there is often a shrewdness about the popular choice.

By contrast, not many tears will be shed over the departure of Ackerman. One lesson of the season is that we underestimated Fouhy – as we continue to underestimate Jeremy Hughes. Until Fouhy returns I should play Hughes and Nigel Rees in the centre with Yeandle on the wing.

The dominating forward of last season was the alarmingly large young flanker Stuart Russell. There were three others who were international prospects, Tim Jones, John Collins and Matthew Watkins. Russell injured himself in the Barbarians match and has since been seen in a fedora hat on the touchline. The others have been playing more or less regularly. The additional absentee has been Collins's fellow lock Ted Lewis. These few enforced changes should not have made the difference they have done. But something has made a difference. Even after their predictable defeat by Bath in the John Player Cup, the Welsh were expected to recapture some of their old glories. They have not done so yet. Like Dr Watson, I confess myself baffled.

HOW BRIGHT ARE THE BLUES?
The Field, November 1985

There is a story that, before the last war, the late W. T. S. Stallybrass, who became Principal of Brasenose College, Oxford,wished to award a special scholarship at the college to an outstanding young rugby player. Stallybrass was an academic lawyer (editor of several editions of *Salmond on Torts*) who was of Continental origin and had adopted a new, more resonant name. He killed himself accidentally by getting out of a railway carriage on the wrong side while returning to Oxford from a legal dinner in London, but that by the way.

Stallybrass's spies, or scouts, were sent forth to scour the schools of the land. They came up with the name of the 18-year-old Wilfred Wooller, of Rydal School. Wooller was summoned for a brief examination. He completed his paper; the examiners met and made their recommendations. There was no place for Wooller. Why not? Stallybrass demanded. He had expressly instructed that the young man was to be awarded a scholarship. The examiners replied that they had considered the matter carefully but could not see their way to awarding a scholarship, even for rugby, to a candidate who thought Jesus was spelled with a G. So Wooller went to Christ's College, Cambridge, instead.

I rather doubt this story myself. Wooller has always struck me as a readable writer and fluent commentator – though of course he may not have been able to spell. A quarter of a century later he helped to get Tony Lewis into the same Cambridge college.

In the always lively and often very funny extracts from his forthcoming sporting autobiography which are appearing in the *Sunday Telegraph*, Lewis writes: 'Probably none of us rugger Blues ... would be admitted ... these days, when admission is strictly linked to high academic performance at A-level....Nowadays, Cambridge University makes no commitment to excellence at games. A dimension of university experience has been firmly removed by the scalpels of the admissions tutors. It is probable that first class cricket and rugby will soon end at Fenners and Grange Road, and the Boat Race will be no more than a spring scuttle between overgrown schoolboys.'

Wooller has said the same kind of thing several times in his occasional notes to the programme for the Oxford and Cambridge match. It is plausible. It is often said. But is it true? The Boat Race has not been the national event it used to be since around 1939. University cricket has tended to come and go: the Cambridge teams – the Cambridge players – of the 1950s were exceptional, not normal. The end of the war generation, and then the end of the National Service generation, meant that undergraduates arrived at the university as boys rather than as young men. This was true of sportsmen generally, as it was true likewise that higher academic standards were expected of them. We now hear a good deal also about the decline of rugby in comprehensive schools, and the reluctance of parents to allow their sons to play the game, owing to its growing reputation for physical danger.

At this point, however, I think we should pause, collect our thoughts and examine the evidence, such as it is. For one thing, the young Tony Lewis, from Neath Grammar School, would almost certainly have got into Cambridge anyway, irrespective of his prowess on the rugby and cricket fields. He is an accomplished writer and a versatile man. These qualities were presumably apparent when he was 17 or 18. As I know to my advantage, the Oxbridge, anyway the Cambridge, admissions tutors, operated a system of positive discrimination many years before that phrase became part of political debate. Anyone from a remote or obscure grammar school who really wanted to get to Cambridge, showed some promise and possessed the basic qualifications for entry was given preference.

For another thing, if Lewis, Wooller and the others believe that the members of the Oxford and Cambridge rugby teams all possess three A grades at A-level, two As and a B or even two Bs and an A, they overestimate the requirements of the colleges. Half the members of the Cambridge team seem to be reading Land Economy, which used to be called Estate Management, I seem to remember. Do not misunderstand me: I am not asserting either that it is a soft option or that those who take it are none too bright. It makes you wonder, however, how and why quite so many rugby players end up as land economists. Perhaps Cambridge has been so much more successful than Oxford in recent years because it offers Land Economy as a subject, whereas Oxford does not.

Indeed, a back division selected from the Cambridge sides of this period could, with the right pack in front of them, take on any international side in the world: H. Davies; S. Smith, K. Simms, F. Clough, M. Bailey; R. Andrew, R. Moon. There are also Marcus Rose, Ian Metcalfe and, from a slightly earlier generation, John Robbie. Oxford could supply Hugo MacNeill, Stuart Barnes and, from an earlier generation likewise, Gareth Davies. The forwards of both universities are less impressive, but then, they usually have been less so, on account of differences of age, strength and roughness between universities and clubs.

It may be that we are seeing a slow decline in the universities, as we have in the services, in the old boys and in the hospitals. Conversely some clubs rise extraordinarily quickly, of which the most recent example is Nottingham. Twenty years ago, however, observers predicted that the universities of the future, in rugby terms, were Loughborough and St Luke's, Exeter. They have disappointed rather – perhaps because they do not offer Land Economy. On the other hand, the polytechnics and the technical institutes have come on. But Oxbridge is still in the lead.

NO CONSOLATION FOR WALES
The Field, December 1985

For the last few seasons Wales have been taking one step forward and two steps back. This would not matter if the team were enjoying themselves, as Ireland manifestly were in 1984–85. It would even be a consolation if the Welsh behaved as the French do or, rather, used to before they turned all responsible – sacking the captain, jettisoning the coach, changing the selectors or dispatching entire teams *à la lanterne*.

Wales, by contrast, have been crabbed and miserable and bad-tempered, both on and off the field. There is something sadly symbolic in the retirement of the coach, John Bevan, through ill-health. His period of authority was, as the Marxists put it, full of internal contradictions. He said he would encourage – nay, insist on – 'running rugby'. His first step towards this happy state of affairs was to get rid of the best stand-off half in the five European countries, Gareth Davies of Cardiff, and to replace him with Malcolm Dacey of Swansea. After some irrational to-ing and fro-ing Davies retired from international rugby in understandable disgust. Whereupon another Davies appeared on the scene, Jonathan of Neath, and out went Dacey.

As it happens, the best Welsh stand-off half I have seen this season (Gareth Davies apart) is Dacey's sidekick at Swansea, Aled Williams, but this by the way. Having selected or, precisely, having failed to make up his mind about the stand-off most conducive to open rugby, Bevan consistently preferred at centre Robert Ackerman, recently of London Welsh, who makes a bull going at a gate look subtle. What rendered it sadder, in a way, was that Bevan seemed entirely sincere. When the Irish coach, Mick Doyle, said last season that he just wanted to throw the ball about and did not care about kicking goals we did not wholly believe him. We thought he was making an Irish joke. And we were right. Ireland won the championship because they had an excellent goal-kicker in Michael Kiernan and the best back five forwards in the competition, who would be in any Lions 30. No one in Wales, by contrast, seems to possess Doyle's clarity or conviction.

The Welsh authorities seem to be behaving in equally unintelligent fashion over international players who are sent off. The most recent example is Robert Norster of Cardiff. Last season, it may be remembered, Steve Bainbridge got himself sent off and was prohibited from playing for England for the entire championship. Wales refused then to adopt the same policy. England accordingly reverted to the old rule of suspension for a period merely. Wales duly adopted the English rule of last season. The two ships, so to speak, passed each other sailing in opposite directions and neglected to exchange signals.

Bainbridge has now been sent off yet again. He seems an impetuous sort of lad. He does not look a ruffian. But then, tall, thin forwards such as Bainbridge are, for no very good reason, assumed to be more innocent characters than short, fat forwards such as, say, Gareth Chilcott of Bath. Anyway, Bainbridge is merely suspended, whereas Norster is out for the season. This is absurd. It is also one of those situations where uniformity and predictability are more important than abstract justice. Home unions do not exact differing penalties for club matches; but it is essential in the international championship. Or, rather, it ought to be essential, for the sake of fairness not only to individual players but also to the competing countries.

Most people would agree, I think, that a general six weeks' suspension is too lax, while a suspension from all internationals is too severe. I should favour a six or possibly eight weeks' suspension from all rugby after a sending-off, together with suspension from the first championship international after the incident and from any additional internationals (if any) preceding the first championship match.

I do not, however, want to be too hard on the Welsh administrators or selectors. Pursuing them is a great national sport, with an even more numerous following than rugby itself. They cannot be blamed for the Terry Holmes affair, though I should have told the scrap-metal merchant to make up his mind one way or another and stop fooling about, causing worry and inconvenience all round. His possible successor, David Bishop of Pontypool, has a disposition to find himself in trouble not only with referees but with the constabulary at large. I should give young Bishop a wide berth.

Though a head of steam is building up behind both Ray Giles of Aberavon and Jonathan Griffiths of Llanelli, the two best scrum-halves after Holmes are Mark Douglas of London Welsh and Robert Jones of Swansea. Douglas is stronger, but Jones is the better footballer. Indeed, he is, in sheer footballing ability – long passes with either hand, the provision of options for his partner – the superior of Holmes as well. I should pick Jones like a shot.

DIVIDED AGAINST ITSELF

The Field, January 1986

I am of the generation to whom Sergeant Pepper means an Australian cricketer rather than a Beatles song. He was one of the overseas services team (which included Calvert, Carmody and, above all, Miller) and, to a small boy in Wales, he exceeded in cricketing glamour all others apart from Denis Compton a few years later on and, naturally, Bradman's 1948 Australians.

Similarly my first acquaintance with rugby, real rugby, was made in the closing years of the last war, at the St Helen's ground, Swansea. These were the days of the wartime service competition and the service internationals. My father took me on the bus from Tycroes, 12 miles away. A schoolmaster, he considered it his privilege to disregard bus queues, then an important part of the business of daily life because of the scarcity of private cars. He also consistently refused to pay my fare on the bus, saying airily to the conductor that I was a 'schoolboy', as if this settled the matter. Once at the ground, we stood on the 'tanner bank', which derived its name from the price originally charged for admission and not, as I thought to begin with, from the famous Swansea and Welsh scrum-half, Haydn Tanner.

But we saw Lieutenant, subsequently Captain, Tanner play, as we saw the English forwards Ray Longland, Joe Mycock, a youthful Bob Weighill and H. B. Toft. Squadron Leader Toft was a particular favourite of my father's owing to his intellectual qualities. Quite why he knew about them at this stage is mysterious, for some years were to pass before Toft established himself with *The Observer* as one of the great post-war rugby writers.

Then there were the Rugby League players, Ernest Ward of England, E.H. (Ted) Ward and Gus Risman of Wales. The greatest of these was undoubtedly Risman, at any rate when, as a League player, he was playing to Union rules, as they all were. He was, however, challenged by the young Flying Officer Bleddyn Williams of RAF St Athan. The argument could go on for hours, happily and inconclusively. Who was the better midfield player, Risman or Williams?

Union and League players can still play together in service sides, even at Twickenham itself, without the Union players' suffering deleterious consequences in their own footballing careers. So can they play together also if they happen to be in one of HM prisons. The wartime period of 40 years ago saw co-operation between the players enriching the Union game. Maybe it enriched the League game too, though I do not know. Why should there not be some such co-operation today?

Writing recently in the *Sunday Telegraph*, Wilfred Wooller implied that Terry Holmes, in going from Cardiff to Bradford Northern, was joining the legions of the damned. Indeed, Wooller did not so much imply it as state it as vigorously as he would, in his cricketing days, have run out a batsman at the bowler's end when he was doing the bowling and the unfortunate batsman had strayed an inch out of his crease. It was not merely, he gave us to understand, that Holmes would be shunned and avoided by right-thinking members of rugby society generally. The freemasonry would also come to an end: not so much the free beer as the good jobs. Jobbery in Rugby Union is a subject with which I hope to deal more fully in another column.

For the moment I will content myself with a story about Nigel Horton and the late Ricky Bartlett, the nicest of men. Horton, Bartlett said, wished to return from France and to be set up in a pub in the London area. If the Harlequins could arrange such a satisfactory outcome, he was in gratitude prepared to play for the club. As it turned out, Horton joined the Wasps, though he did not play very often or for very long. Much, much worse: the Welsh wing John Bevan, a schoolmaster in a small way of business, was told when he went north not to expect any jobs when and if he returned to Wales. Many such practices are probably illegal. But so also may be the discrimination practised by the Union against their former players who have gone to the League and now wish to make some contribution to their first game. David Watkins and Ray French are examples.

The former Oxford and England wing Derek Wyatt has

already suggested that dissatisfied persons should take their case to the European Court of Human Rights. I should be inclined to try before a domestic court first, for the Union authorities are on shaky ground. They do not object to professional sportsmen as such: Alastair Hignell, Dusty Hare and Peter Squires are all professional cricketers who played amateur rugby for England. The Union objection is to another – though not a wholly different – game, to a set of rules or laws. But the Union is not a private club. Through the Sports Council it receives public money. And the real remedy may have to be political rather than legal.

FRANCE FOR CHAMPIONS
The Field, January 1986

For a decade or so now people have been saying how dreadful British rugby is. When it is not dull it is dirty and when it is not dirty it is dull. There is some truth in this. Still, I see signs that the international season which is now starting will turn out better than some recent ones. The new laws about front row play seem to be making collapsed scrums less frequent. The laws about tackle and release have certainly added to fluency. The latter changes ought to favour France for the championship. My money is on them, though unhappily the bookmakers agree with me (as they did not last season, when I supported Ireland).

The great hope which other countries always have – or used to have – about the French is that they become easily demoralised. This British view (for it extended beyond England) was chauvinistic but nonetheless remained broadly true until the 1950s. Yet, though the French may no longer give up on the field, they can certainly fall out when they are off it. The coach, Jacques Fouroux, is clearly an awkward customer. He intends to persist with the scrum-half's throwing-in of the ball at the lineout, a ploy which seems to me more sensible than some other observers appear to think. In this respect the French are ahead of fashion.

In the same respect – throwing-in at the lineout – they used to be behind fashion until quite recently. They continued using the wing to do the job as in olden times. Moreover, some of the finest three-quarters in the world would throw in underarm and two-handed. This was the only kind of throw I ever mastered. It was rather looked down on even 30 years ago. There is a moral here somewhere. It is perhaps that you do not always have to be absolutely up-to-date to be successful.

There is seldom much risk of that where Scotland are concerned, though. I feel sorry for the selectors, who had an even more wretched final trial than their first choices. Some of my readers, I hear, claim I am unfair to Scotland, writing too much, too often about England and Wales, the latter particularly. I plead guilty but advance extenuating circumstances. Welsh clubs are continually coming to England, London especially. Scottish clubs come rarely; likewise clubs from the north of England. Even full-time London-based rugby correspondents hardly ever stray north of Nottingham. If they want an outing, they prefer to go to Dublin.

My prediction is that Ireland will be in the upper part of the middle, above Scotland but below France. They will miss Keith Crossan and Nigel Carr in their first match (with France). Ciaran Fitzgerald may not be the best hooker in the world or even in the home countries. He is manifestly worth his place as a captain, if you believe, as I do, that captaincy is a skill for which a player can be specifically chosen.

England, by contrast, have gone round the houses and into the wood. The season began with David Cooke of Harlequins the favourite for the captaincy. Poor Cooke finds himself not even in the team, Peter Winterbottom of Headingley being preferred both to him and to the even unluckier Gary Rees of Nottingham. Rees was perhaps the outstanding player, Huw Davies apart, in the successful divisional championship – which envious and ill-disposed persons from the south-west are now depreciating. Anyway, Cooke having been eliminated at an intermediate stage, there was a consequential hum for Maurice Colclough, now of Swansea. In the end the job does not go to Davies, the best choice, but to Nigel Melville, also of

Wasps. Courageously though he has overcome injury, he is an even more fragile player than Terry Holmes. And yet England might surprise us all. This is a hunch; no more.

Wales need only one further season without winning the championship to equal that other fallow period, 1957-63. Then they went seven years without claiming the title. Today it is six years. In the pre-1957 period one has to go back to 1923-30 for a more barren patch. Admittedly the selectors and administrators have been as maladroit as any MCC sub-committee in putting up the backs of reasonable men – Jeff Squire, Graham Price, Gareth Davies and, most recently, Gwyn Evans (they should not be blamed for Mike Watkins's defection).

The truth is still that a Lions Test side could now be assembled that did not contain a single Welshman. Even such fine players as the foolishly barred Robert Norster and the still flourishing David Pickering would find themselves challenged for places.

Wales may be becoming underdogs again – as Australia have become underdogs at cricket yet top dogs at rugby. We may have to revise our lists of top and underdogs. France have been at or near the top for some time. I still take them to win the championship.

TIME FOR A CHANGE IN THE RULES
The Field, February 1986

My friend and colleague Geoffrey Wheatcroft is a great one for changing the rules. By this I do not mean that he behaves as Arthur Scargill and Margaret Thatcher are disposed to do when confronted by a difficulty. *Au contraire*, as Lord George-Brown used to say. What I mean is that Wheatcroft likes to think up improvements to the rules, in politics as much as in rugby football. Why, he asks, should there be 650 MPs? Would we not be better off with 350 instead? My usual response to this kind of (perfectly sensible) question is to say that we can waste all day speculating about desirable changes and must take the world as it is.

And yet ... rules *are* changed, in rugby football as much as in politics. Or, to be precise, they are changed more frequently and drastically in rugby. Rule-changes in politics are slow and bitterly contested because they are almost always to one group's advantage, another's disadvantage – and are clearly seen to be so. There is a lot to be said for 'interest' in this sense. Its workings inhibit irresponsibility. The rugby authorities, by contrast, make and unmake the rules virtually every season: sometimes, it seems, just for the fun of it. Like most Welshmen, by the way, I naturally talk about 'the rules' rather than 'the laws'. 'Rules' is, I think, a more accurate word for what we are discussing. But hereinafter I shall reluctantly follow English usage and write about 'the laws'.

The Scotland and Wales match may perhaps go down in the history of the game as the one after which people looked at one another, shook their heads and said: this nonsense has gone too far and must stop. For the first time since 1887, when Wales also won (it was against Ireland), a side scoring one try in a home championship match beat a side scoring three. Moreover, if Gavin Hastings had been successful with all his kicks, including conversions, and Paul Thorburn unsuccessful with his, Scotland would have beaten Wales 27-7.

There is, admittedly, a kind of rough justice to what has happened in the international season so far. Rather, injustice has been dispensed with a fair degree of impartiality. Scotland beat France through Hastings's boot alone; England beat Wales mainly through Rob Andrew. Hastings was off form at Cardiff, whereas Thorburn was firmly on it. Indeed, he had been even more consistent, though less spectacular, at Twickenham earlier, when he kicked four out of four. At this mid-stage he is my nomination for player of the season, despite strong competition from Wade Dooley and John Jeffrey.

Nor is it coincidence that the 'personalities' of contemporary rugby are chiefly kickers of goals. The match between Ireland and France was dominated not by the play of the last

72

stages but by the boots of Guy Laporte and Michael Kiernan, who took the only three chances the French offered him. They had earlier had the Riot Act, or whatever is its French equivalent, read to them by Jacques Fouroux.

One of the many paradoxes of the new laws, designed among other things to discourage rucking, is that they put a premium on players staying on their feet. Yet the New Zealanders, the greatest exponents – virtually the inventors – of rucking, insist on players staying on their feet while engaging in the activity. In fact an upright or semi-upright posture is of its essence. Though they *can* lead to more flowing play, the laws have not on the whole been a success.

Another difficulty is that they try to render the scrum less dangerous by compelling the referee to make impossible judgements. Often the other forwards themselves do not know whether Jones is dragging Smith down or Smith pushing Jones down. At the same time the laws make scrums more probable and more frequent. It would be more sensible to make the wheeled scrum illegal. By its very nature it places players offside. I should also prohibit the brutish and potentially lethal massed forward rush for the line which the Scots tried out three times against Wales and from which, I was glad to see, they did not score – though they claim they did.

I should get rid of the mark too. And I see no reason why modern, fit players should be able to kick direct into touch from behind their 25-yard (or, as Nigel Starmer-Smith insists on calling it, 22-metre) line.

The solution lies in reserving the penalty-kick for serious and deliberate offences. Other offences would be penalised with either a scrum or a kick direct to touch at the discretion of the wronged side. In these circumstances the value of the kick should, I think, stay at three. But I should increase the drop to four points and decrease the conversion to one. Wheatcroft's solution is simply to abolish the place-kick entirely. But then, he is more radical than I am.

THE TROUBLE WITH 'TOTAL RUGBY'

The Field, March 1986

'Total football' was a phrase that first became popular, as I remember, slightly more than a decade ago. It was used about soccer rather than rugby, in particular about the Dutch soccer team. It meant that every player could if necessary do every other player's job (except, presumably, the goalkeeper's). Specialisation was no longer to be absolute. The ball was to do the work. Moreover, the players were intelligent, with university degrees, that kind of thing – though whether this last was a useful bonus or a necessary part of the new scheme of things was not wholly clear.

After Scotland's splendid win over England several people have started to talk about 'total rugby' in rather the same way. Forwards should be able to play like backs and, though perhaps to a lesser extent, backs like forwards. Speed to the breakdown, quickness with the pass and, above all, stamina on the field are the essence of this style, which some observers trace to the 1984 Australians, others to the New Zealanders.

Fewer commentators have mentioned the French. In fact they have been playing off and on in this fashion for the last 30 years. Scotland are supposed to have played similarly on 15 February. I write 'supposed to' not to depreciate the Scots but to urge caution in the use of phrases such as 'total rugby', 'the Australian style', 'the New Zealand style' or whatever. Scotland were enabled to play reminiscently of New Zealand partly because the referee, Bob Francis, came from there. And, after all, the domination of New Zealand with South African rugby before the 1970s was a consequence of the domination of their forwards. We beat them at the beginning of that decade, as we cannot beat them now, because we took them on in front.

Nevertheless, having entered this *caveat*, we know roughly what we mean. Scotland had seven athletes in their pack. The exception was Iain Milne, and he has other qualities. But Colin Deans, the captain, is as fast as many centres. Alex Brewster, the replacement loose-head prop, is a converted international flanker. Iain Paxton, a lock, is a converted international and Lions No 8.

The back row needs no introduction, as the boxing posters of my youth used to put it when they could not think of anything else to say about the contender. There is plenty to say about John Jeffrey, John Beattie and Finlay Calder. I shall desist, because a lot has been said already, and turn instead to the England forwards.

They numbered among them only two who could be considered athletes in the Scottish sense: Peter Winterbottom and Steve Brain. But Brain, though a former back, is not as fast as Deans; while Winterbottom seems to spend much of his life on the ground, flat on his face, doing no good to anyone, least of all himself. After the Welsh match Wade Dooley was being acclaimed with some astonishment as an athlete too, chiefly – so it seems in retrospect – on account of Welsh incompetence at the lineout. No such claims are being advanced on his behalf after the Scottish match.

Maurice Colclough, on the other hand, is quite athletic considering his great size. I felt sorry for him when two Scottish tries came indirectly from his endeavours. The pass of his which Rob Andrew failed to take was certainly not a perfect one. But it was not wholly bad either. It was too hard, too fast and delivered from too great a height. Other stand-off halves would have caught it. But then, Colclough is one of those players who are always being blamed.

As far as their forwards go, Wales are nearer to England than to Scotland, Billy James and Pickering being the equivalents of Brain and Winterbottom. Ireland, Nigel Carr restored, but still missing Philip Matthews for the Welsh match, are nearer to Scotland, even though they deservedly lost on 15 February.

Before we become carried away by all this talk of athleticism and total rugby, however, we should remember that one of the glories of the game has always been that a boy who was neither a natural athlete nor a natural ballplayer could nonetheless aspire to the highest honours, as he could not in most other sports. Usually such ambitions were restricted to those who were very tall, very heavy or both.

This commendable opportunity which rugby offered the

less physically gifted had, however, its obverse side, which came to preponderate. In the past 25 years or so it has become a game for freaks, among forwards at any rate. Now it is not so much that if one is tall, heavy or both and there is still a chance of advancement irrespective of one's footballing, qualities – which is admirable. Rather it is that to advance at all in six or seven out of eight places in the pack one has to be tall, heavy or both, irrespective of whether one can play football or not – which is a different matter.

In the successful Welsh side of the early 1950s the props, John Robins and the late Cliff Davies, were both less than five foot ten and 14 stone. The locks, Rees Stephens and the late Roy John, were respectively six foot two and 15 stone and six foot four and 13½ stone. Today they would have to be flankers, in which position John would be told he was on the light side. It is all very well to say that forwards have grown bigger. Backs have not grown commensurately with forwards. If England's defeat brings about the demise of the freak forward, I shall certainly be happier, total rugby or not.

THE SILLY STATE OF THE TABLE
The Field, March 1986

'France first, the rest nowhere,' said Alan Pryce-Jones. The distinguished former editor of *The Times Literary Supplement* said this on the feature pages of a Sunday newspaper several years ago. He was, as it happens, talking about food. On the evidence of the season, I echo him on rugby too.

Nor has it been France's most glittering season of recent years by any means. Blanco has not been on his best form, Laporte has been consistently undistinguished, Codorniou has not been playing, and Gallion and, more recently, Estève have been dropped.

Lafond appears to have solved France's recent problems on the other wing and is, I hazard, better at English than any British Isles wing is at French. When complimented on television by Nigel Starmer-Smith on one of his two tries against Wales, he replied modestly: 'It is not difficult to run after a ball.' When asked why the French backs were so good, he explained simply: 'We practise together.'

This is not, admittedly, a wholly satisfactory explanation. The English backs practise like anything and still exhibit their traditional failing of stopping, sticking a finger in their mouths and asking themselves: 'Now what am I supposed to do next?' Anyway, Lafond apart, the only established French back who has enhanced his reputation is Sella. (This implies no disrespect to Charvet and Bonneval, who were largely unknown in this country.)

And yet, France have looked in a different class. They should have beaten Scotland. But then, Scotland should have beaten Wales, and Wales England. Though Ireland have been a bit unlucky at times, they cannot really complain about being bottom of the table. As things have turned out, Wales's bad luck against England was their good luck against Scotland. Their tally of two wins out of four is just. Scotland have likewise been justly treated by fate or whatever; two out of three is I think the right ratio.

What is justice? What indeed! Still, an equitable international table would at this stage be in the order: first, France, then Scotland and Wales (Wales with four points from four matches, Scotland with four from three), followed by England and, last, Ireland. It really is dotty that England could now win the championship outright if they were to beat France and Scotland were defeated by – even simply managed to draw with – Ireland.

Before the season began I wrote that England might surprise us all. But I thought then that, if they did, they would do so with more vim, zip, drive, pep, initiative and, in the last resort, sheer physical fitness than they have in fact displayed. The silly state of the international table is the consequence of two matches, Scotland-France and England-Wales, and of two players, respectively Gavin Hastings and Rob Andrew. It is the consequence of penalty goals. Paul Thorburn has been even more consistent than Hastings. But his enormous contribution has not had the same effect on the shape of the table.

A lot has already been written on this subject. I shall not go over churned-up ground again. Indeed, the wonder is that the table is not even more skewed than it is. A greater wonder still is that we have seen so much attractive rugby, from – in order of attractiveness – France, Scotland, Wales and occasionally Ireland, but not, alas, from England. This is what makes the current table so unfair.

The received wisdom of the moment is that England might be in an even more favourable position – might have beaten Scotland, which I rather doubt myself – if they had played to their strengths at Murrayfield, not spreading the ball, keeping the game tight. And they did, after all, score four tries against Ireland, something virtually unheard of by their sides in recent years.

But two of these tries were push overs. One was a penalty try from a potential push over. And the fourth, by Huw Davies, was the consequence of an Irish defensive kicking error and an even bigger mistake when he was allowed to twist, turn and roll his way over the line. The best try was the one by Mike Harrison that was disallowed. I was glad for Davies, nevertheless. He had played courageously against Scotland. He was not responsible for the defeat. There was no reason to drop him in favour of Marcus Rose, which seemed to be in the selectors' minds at one time.

All in all the English backs, in contrast to the forwards, have been treated cavalierly by the selectors. Simon Smith had not let the side down. Jamie Salmon did all that could have been asked of him – or all that he was allowed to do – in the Scottish match. His round-the-neck tackle of Roger Baird in that game, from which Scotland were awarded a penalty, was both necessary and fair, unless it is held that *any* high tackle is dangerous. If the referee believed this in the particular circumstances of Salmon tackling Baird, his proper course was to award a penalty try.

In the pack, Dean Richards and Gary Rees should have been included from the beginning. But it is madness, in response to the call for greater mobility among the forwards, to retain Gareth Chilcott, Gary Pearce and Wade Dooley. I certainly expect the French to run them all round the Parc des Princes. In that case some justice will have been done. But I shall still be pleased if Scotland share the championship with France.

IRELAND'S MISSED OPPORTUNITIES
The Field, April 1986

One of the most affecting moments of the international championship occurred when Michael Kiernan missed a conversion kick against Scotland that would have given Ireland the match, while Tony Ward looked on. But then the Irish – selectors as much as players – are adept at providing little touches of this kind. Many may recall the occasion a few years ago when a middle-aged Tony O'Reilly turned up on the wing at Twickenham, a fantasy from the *Boys Own Paper* or, rather, *The Director*.

Players seem to go on for longer, winning more caps, than those of other countries, as if they were the rugby equivalents of the allegedly ancient citizens of Georgia in the USSR. In Ireland the recall is mightier than the drop, as Phil Orr among many has demonstrated. I am surprised that the Irish did not bring back John O'Driscoll either in place of the injured Philip Matthews (whom they missed throughout the season) or as No 8 when Brian Spillane unexpectedly and unjustly fell from favour.

Ireland have had an unlucky season but a good – or a lucky – decade. They have won or shared the championship three times since 1980, as many times as France and once more than Scotland. They won the Triple Crown in 1982 and 1985, though they have won the Grand Slam only once in their history, in 1948. They are quite capable of winning it again in 1987. In Mick Doyle they have the best coach in the four countries. He would be the automatic choice as coach or manager of any current Lions team. Or rather, he is so accomplished that he would probably be left out altogether, so obtuse has the British Isles management policy been for the last decade.

But Doyle's shifts – in the meaning both of changes and of expedients – have not altogether made sense this season. Take the forwards first. Having cleared out the house a few years ago and sent some of the older, heavier pieces off to the saleroom, coach and selectors alike should have made do with, and even cherished, the new furniture. Admittedly, both Matthews and Nigel Carr were unavailable to begin with. This put a premium on retaining the rest of the pack.

Instead the Irish fiddled around. A front row of Des Fitzgerald, Ciaran Fitzgerald and Paul Kennedy is not manifestly superior to one of J. J. McCoy, Ciaran Fitzgerald and Orr. Indeed there are some armchair front row forwards who would maintain that, as Fitzgerald is not the best hooker in the home countries, so equally he is not the best in Ireland. Certainly W. Ryan was impressive on the recent Barbarians tour of Wales.

Nor is it by any means self-evident that Brian McCall is a better partner than Willie Anderson for Donal Lenihan at lock. Everyone knows that the main problems are in the front row: at hooker, where one has to do what is now called a trade-off between Fitzgerald's inspirational qualities and his technical deficiencies, and at loose-head, where age is inevitably catching up with Orr, and Kennedy does not look altogether the player to take his place.

Injury to Paul Dean and Keith Crossan affected the backs too. But here there seems to have been more consistency in selection. It is fashionable among my colleagues to say or write that Hugo MacNeill is 'not the fastest thing on two legs'. He appeared fast enough to me when he put Trevor Ringland in for that splendid first-half try against Wales.

Ringland ends the season as the second most impressive wing in the home championship – on the evidence of the matches themselves. Matt Duncan was the most impressive but Rory Underwood was simply not given the chance to show he was the best of the lot. Brendan Mullin has a touch of genius and would be in most people's British Isles team. Crossan seems to have recovered well from his broken jaw.

Rugby memories are, however, short: not so short as soccer memories, not so long as cricket's. Only two years have passed since Ollie Campbell last played for Ireland. In Doyle's place I should have tried to play him and Ward together, whether as full-back and stand-off half or as stand-off and centre. The adoption of a settled policy of playing inside and outside centres, with either Ward or Campbell inside, and the other at stand-off half, could have kept them both in the side throughout the early 1980s, as could the transformation of either into a full-back.

But Ward annoyed the Irish authorities; partly, it is said, by posing in one of our tabloid papers in scanty attire as a kind of page three rugby footballer. Campbell, for his part, has been both injured and ill. That pale look of his was not entirely deceptive. It is now too late to bring them together, even if the Irish authorities wished to do so. Watching Ward, himself watching the usually admirable Kiernan, a few weeks ago, I felt a twinge not exactly of sadness but rather of retrospective regret at what might have been. For the 1980s have been not only Ireland's decade but also one in which they have denied us the privilege of seeing two of their greatest players either individually or – what would have been better still – together.

GENERAL REFLECTIONS OF A WATCHER
The Field, April 1986

I am sure we have heard enough about the international season. Here are some reflections of a rugby watcher about 1985-86 more generally.

The relative success was the divisional championship, though people from the west complained because they did not win it. When I write that it was a success, I mean no more than that spectators, Press, players and administrators were reasonably enthusiastic. They were not simply going through the motions. As successive trials for the England side, however, the matches were a source of error.

Thus the Midlands selectors preferred Graham Robbins to

Dean Richards at No 8. Richards was then apparently excluded initially from international consideration. The England position went to Robbins, a very ordinary club player, his three tries in the county final notwithstanding (though much the same may be said of his equivalent in the Welsh side, Phil Davies).

Contrariwise, the selectors refused to follow the evidence of the competition when it came to flankers. Gary Rees was not only the outstanding flanker of the matches but the outstanding player. Yet he, like Richards, was brought into the England side halfway through the season. This, however, is not meant to be another why-oh-why article about the England team. All I say is that the divisional championship justified itself as a source always of rugby interest, sometimes of rugby spectacle.

I wish I could say the same of the county championship. Or, to be honest: if the county championship were constantly interesting and spectacular, I doubt whether I could summon up much enthusiasm for it. How many people really cared that Warwickshire beat Kent on 12 April? No one I met, anyway. It is, I suppose, good for rugby that the usually despised Kent are in a final of any kind. But in a way this demonstrated what a silly competition it is. Both Blackheath and Coventry, the clubs from whom the finalists drew – and would expect to draw – the bulk of their teams are wasted versions of their old selves.

The best clubs in England are now, in no particular order, Nottingham, Leicester, Bath and Wasps. One would expect their pre-eminence to be reflected in a properly organised county championship, even allowing for the luck of the draw. But it is not so. The county championship is now an untidy irrelevance, buried, as Marx might have put it, in the dustbin of history. English rugby will not do justice to its talent until primacy is given to the clubs.

The John Player Cup now attracts interest and enthusiasm, though it has taken a long time for it to do so. The merit tables, by contrast, are a mess. The existence of the John Smith table, and the London table – not to mention tables concocted by various newspapers – make them even more of a mess. There is an easy solution. It is to think in terms of leagues rather than of tables. Anglo-Welsh fixtures would be retained, even encouraged, as would Anglo-Scottish and Anglo-Irish fixtures, of which last two categories there are, I think, too few. Every other first class match in England would be a league match, apart from Barbarian or other festival fixtures. The London exile clubs would be invited to participate. The league would have three divisions, or possibly two divisions with the second divided into north and south. The only thing wrong with this idea is that it is not going to happen, so entrenched are the opposing interests. So I shall conclude with some prizes.

The outstanding club were Cardiff, whose pack were somewhat superior to the Welsh one. Indeed, they possessed five flankers, any two of whom would not disgrace a Lions XV: Owen Golding, Bob Lakin, Terry Charles, Gareth Roberts and Tim Crothers. Crothers was the best flanker I saw this season. I am not forgetting Rees or John Jeffrey either. And Crothers cannot secure a regular place in the Cardiff side.

The luckiest player was Fran Clough, who is of the same type as Simon Halliday but not his clear superior in any major respect. Other lucky players were Phil Lewis and Phil Davies. The most disappointing player was David Pickering. The most exciting players, Frenchmen apart, were Jonathan Davies and Robert Jones; the most unjustly treated, Simon Smith and Jamie Salmon. The most grotesque was Gareth Chilcott. The most promising was Paul Moriarty, who, alas, seems to have more than a touch of his brother Richard's temper.

The most disappointing clubs were those I watch most frequently, London Welsh and Harlequins. John Olver is, I think, the best hooker in England. He has Iain Milne on one side of him, Paul Curtis on the other and, behind him, Cuthbertson, O'Brien, Skinner, Jackson (or Butcher) and Cooke – the unluckiest player of the season. Yet Quins dominate only when they come up against powder-puff packs.

London Welsh are not such a disappointment because they

do not have the players. I recommend, however, that the English selectors keep an eye on their stand-off half, Colyn Price, who has a dual qualification and has, like Huw Davies and Stuart Barnes, opted for England. Barnes at full-back, Davies at centre and Price as stand-off might work not wonders but something for England next season.

CHARLES BURGESS AND OTHERS

In January 1986 Stephen Glover invited me to lunch with him at Sweetings in the City. He was one of the three journalists from the *Daily Telegraph* – Matthew Symonds and Andreas Whittam Smith were the others – who had left that paper to found *The Independent*. The new paper was now reasonably certain to be launched, though that certainty did not become absolute until a few more months had passed. Glover wished to sound me out about the prospects of my joining or, at the least, contributing to the new enterprise.

I had met and liked Glover, who had that carefree, even indolent air which I find sympathetic. He was a *Telegraph* friend of the former parliamentary sketch-writer Frank Johnson; Johnson and I and Matthew Engel (also represented in this series) had until 1984 occupied separate flats on succeeding storeys of a house in Islington. This arrangement had come about by chance, but Johnson and I had become friends (Engel had arrived on the scene later on). I had met Glover several times in Johnson's ground-floor flat.

I now told him, over lunch, that I was perfectly happy writing my political column in *The Observer*. Nor could I write about politics for his new paper, because my contract with *The Observer* prevented me from doing so. In any case, one's stock of ideas was limited, about politics or anything else. However, I went on, my opportunities for freelance work outside politics were wider than most people seemed to suppose. I wished the new paper well and was keen to help it in any way I could. Glover suggested: What about sport? I distinctly remember him saying 'sport' rather than 'rugby'. I may have replied that, while I could make a reasonable stab at cricket, and knew something about boxing, rugby was the one game where I was surefooted. I did not add that tennis, athletics and golf bored me. At all events, we settled on rugby, and parted with mutual expressions of goodwill.

The next stage was for me to meet the sports editor. He was Charles Burgess, who had come from *The Guardian*: in his early 30s, large, curly-haired, with laughing yet simultaneously dangerous green-blue eyes. His father was a newspaper entrepreneur from Carlisle who had been knighted. Charlie was one of those journalists who, as I subsequently discovered, did not draw any distinction between heavy and light newspapers or – to put it more precisely – did not claim any superiority for the former over the latter.

His vision of my column was that it should be free of the imprimatur of 'the Wing-Commander'. This officer, though loosely modelled on that higher-ranking Air Force figure Bob Weighill, was fictitious, being Burgess's hypostatisation of the administration of the Rugby Union, as the English Rugby Union perhaps somewhat conceitedly call themselves. He expected me to get around the clubhouses and talk to players and officials, he explained: but he did not want me to represent official views, as full-time rugby writers had to do quite properly from time to time. In fact I am reluctant to approach players unless they make it clear that they wish to speak to me, because they are most of them so very young, because it is easy for someone of my age to be a bore or a 'heavy', as some of them say, and because rugby is still an amateur game, and young men prefer to talk to other young men – or to young women. The most popular subject of conversation seems to be curry, and where to obtain it.

But broadly we were at one, as we have happily remained ever since. Burgess's view was that I should represent, in his phrase, 'the intelligent punter', the man in the stand, on the touchline or sitting at home in front of the television set. Indeed, in journalism, only television itself is approached in this way. Admittedly other rugby journalists often write about other things: for instance, that prince among phrase-makers, Christopher Wordsworth, sparkles with equal brightness in the literary pages of *The Guardian* and *The Observer*. But the *Independent* column was deliberately written from the standpoint of an enthusiastic amateur. I was sometimes mistaken, or plain wrong: but I never, I think, pretended to a knowledge which I did not possess.

Now, how would I feel if a full-time rugby writer were plonked down next to me in the Press gallery of the House of Commons and I were told: 'This is old so-and-so. He has always taken a close interest in politics, and he has read a few books on the subject. And he always watches the political programmes on television. He'll be writing a column every week when Parliament is sitting, giving his own impressions of what's going on.'? I like to think that I should welcome the appointment and give the newcomer any help I could. But I cannot be sure; still less am I sure of the response which my colleagues in the Press gallery would make.

The rugby staff of *The Independent* when I started in October 1986 were, however, friendliness itself. They could not have been more helpful. This may have been because we all came from 10 miles or so of one another: Geoffrey Nicholson from Swansea, Tim Glover and Steve Bale from Neath, I from Ammanford. Even so, Welshmen are not famous for getting on well together. But Nicholson I already knew, both from *The Observer*, where he had been No 2 to Clem Thomas, and from his membership of the *galère* who had originated in the Swansea of the 1950s, who had moved to London and who included Kingsley Amis, Nicholson's wife Mavis, and the late John Morgan (commemorated in this section) and his wife Mary.

My greatest debt is to someone else from Swansea, Clem Thomas. Perhaps I should not say Swansea but Brynamman, for that is where he comes from, a village at the top of the Amman Valley, at the start of that magical road to Llangadog, which you climb with the menacing Black Mountains of north-east Carmarthenshire on either side of you, until you surmount a brow and turn a corner, and there, spread before you, is the whole Towy Valley, set out like an 18th-century landscape. Clem, like Charlie, understood the purpose of the column: that it was intended to be, as he put it, 'eccentric', the work of someone who loved the game even though he might not know everything there was to know about it and might not have been much of a player himself (though, as I do not want to be unduly modest, the last limitation applies to many full-time rugby writers as well).

I can only say that Thomas behaved to me as another Welshman, the late Sir Trevor Evans of the *Daily Express*, did when I attended my first TUC in 1960: buying me drinks, finding me seats, introducing me to colleagues and performers, and – most flattering of all – asking my opinion. Clem has even been known to ask me who scored the crucial try. I am grateful to him.

BISHOP SILENCE WOULD BE GOLDEN

The Independent, October 1986

Immediately after his acquittal at the Old Bailey a few years ago, Jeremy Thorpe went round to Lord Goodman and said: 'Right, we're going to sue them all,' listing those papers which had assumed or implied his guilt. Goodman replied that Thorpe was a very lucky man, that he would be most imprudent to re-open the case in any way, and that, if he chose to take this course, he, the greatest solicitor since Cicero, would have nothing whatever to do with the matter.

David Bishop, of Pontypool, reminds me rather of Jeremy Thorpe. True, the cases are not exactly parallel. Thorpe was acquitted, whereas Bishop was convicted, and sentenced to a month's imprisonment, suspended on appeal. Hardly had the pugilistic scrum-half emerged from the law courts when Pontypool were playing him in their first team, to the applause of the local populace. The Welsh Rugby Union have now suspended him for the rest of the season. Bishop has said that he may appeal to the courts and, if necessary, to the European Court of Human Rights.

It was right that he should have been prosecuted for assaulting an opponent while the latter was being held on the ground. Commentators who suggest that this kind of action is par for the course, goes on all the time, and should be overlooked do neither the game nor themselves any service at all. It was right also that the sentence of imprisonment, which was too severe, should have been suspended. And it was right that the WRU took the action it did. Justice had been done, even though mainly by chance, and a period of silence on Bishop's part would now be welcome.

There are, however, a few little doubts bobbing about at the back of my mind. They derive mainly from my conviction that, if the rugby authorities can get something wrong, they will. Most sports bodies are the same. Just as journalists make rotten trade unionists, so sporting administrators make rotten lawyers. If there is a mess to be got into, they will get into it. We may remember the MCC, South Africa and Basil d'Oliveira – or the way in which Mr Justice Slade blew the MCC out of the water in the Kerry Packer case. Only this week Lord's made fools of themselves again, this time over Phil Edmonds, and the Football Association were standing on their heads at the behest of Mrs Thatcher, or appearing so to do.

Bishop's case is not that he has been 'punished already' but that the ban is too long. He was expecting eight to 12 weeks. Anyone listening to him or Ray Prosser might be forgiven for thinking that every first class Welsh club contained at least one player who had, like him, been convicted of assault and was playing merrily away, having served a brief period of suspension.

It is evident to me that, over the years, on and off the field, Bishop has indeed brought the game into disrepute. But, in this most recent case, is he being suspended for assaulting a player? Or for being convicted of assaulting a player? Presumably the latter. This is the core of Bishop's case, though he has not exposed it to the public gaze very clearly. He admits the rugby offence and accepts the usual punishment, which would be a suspension of, say, 12 weeks. But he goes on to say that he is being given an additional – a cruel and unusual – punishment, a whole season's suspension, simply because of the fortuitous circumstance that the assault was made the subject of a criminal prosecution.

There is something else which troubles me. Bringing the game into disrepute is rather like public mischief, insulting behaviour or conduct prejudicial to good order and service discipline. It is useful, we need it, but it can be abused. I do not think it has been abused in the Bishop case. But the logic of the WRU's position is that the game can be brought into disrepute off as well as on the field. Paul Simpson of Bath recently pleaded guilty to assault and was fined £125. The Bath secretary said that, as the episode occurred neither on the field nor on club premises, the club had no further interest in the matter.

I am not calling for Simpson's head, but the principle cannot seriously be maintained. There is no private life and public life. The Welsh Rugby Union are, however, applying the distinction to Richard Moriarty. Moriarty has been suspended several times for foul play on the field. Yet Moriarty is captain of Swansea and the likely captain of Wales. They say that responsibility has worked wonders for the boy. Certainly he was on his best behaviour when I saw him at Twickenham last Saturday. He might nevertheless look at Bishop and say: 'There, but for the grace of God, go I.'

TIME TO STEER A MIDDLE COURSE
The Independent, October 1986

For the first 18 years of my life, all the first class rugby I watched was either at Stradey Park, Llanelli, or at St Helen's, Swansea, with occasional expeditions to Cardiff for the internationals. In those post-war days, a gate of 10,000 was common for an ordinary club match, while double that number would turn out for the visit of the great Cardiff side.

In retrospect, what was most striking about those years was not the quality of the football, which could often be grindingly dull, with the packs plodding in the drizzle up and down the touchline following a mighty kick by the full-back or a shorter one by the scrum-half. No, what was impressive was the scholarship and discernment displayed by the spectators, who seemed prematurely and permanently middle-aged (as indeed most of them were, mining exacting an early physical penalty).

It was disputed whether the Swansea or the Llanelli supporters were the more knowledgeable. On the whole Llanelli's were considered the more *sérieux*, Swansea being by comparison a cosmopolitan, fly-by-night, even raffish kind of place. I see them now, ranging (for it is a mistake to suppose that class distinctions do not exist in Wales) from the miners in their off-duty uniform of single-breasted fawn mackintosh, white artificial silk scarf and flat cap to the more prosperous voters in the stand, schoolmasters and suchlike, in heavy double-breasted overcoat, Paisley or striped scarf, trilby hat and leather gloves, looking like members of the Supreme Soviet about to take the salute at a May Day parade.

By these latter citizens a scrum was judged as if it were a sermon, a prop as a preacher. Though a forward pass might be forgiven, a dropped pass was a sin; while penalty-kicks were the work of the Lord, just or vengeful depending on the side you were supporting.

It was all a bit exhausting. Rather as young French persons get fed up with the fuss their elders make about food and drink, and in reaction want nothing more than Coca-Cola and a McDonald's hamburger, so some of us would say to our fathers, uncles or teachers: 'It's only a game. It's only a lot of men running and kicking a ball about.' Our elders would not shake their heads and wonder where they had gone wrong but, if they were intelligent, agree: 'It is only a game, you're right.' However intelligent they might be, they would rarely add: 'But it's all we've got to talk about, our sole interest in life.' They would never add: 'And it's all we've got to be proud about too, the only activity in which we can take on the rest of the world with a fair chance of beating them, the English especially.'

Oppressive though this high seriousness could be, it was nonetheless a fault on the right side. One did not have to regard rugby as religion to feel ashamed of the behaviour of the crowd at Twickenham last Saturday, when the English XV (in reality England) played Japan. Young people were much in evidence, shirtsleeved or even more scantily attired. However, there were no huge tins of beer being passed around, for on entry to the ground our bags were searched for contraband liquor – something that had never happened to me before at a rugby match.

Drunkenness was not the problem. Nor was it boorishness in the crude sense. Rather it was ignorance, pure ignorance. The spectators tried to be indulgent to the Japanese and severe with the English. In fact they were treating the game as an exhibition match which England were bound to win. The constant cries of 'run it', the booing that broke out when Stuart Barnes and (later, more successfully) Marcus Rose took kicks at goal, were not only tiresome but foolishly patronising to both sides. The Japanese ran the ball as often as they did because, sensibly, they did not wish to concede a lineout with England to throw in. When Mark Bailey on the right wing dropped the ball, loud applause broke out, for no reason that I could discern.

Of course rugby is to be enjoyed. It is arguable that the cheerful ignorance of the Twickenham crowd is preferable to the brutish partisanship displayed by supporters of some West Country sides, notably Bath and Gloucester: interestingly, neither of these cities possesses a League soccer team. But there is a middle course. After last Saturday I feel that what England now need is not so much a new team as some new supporters.

A NEW SLANT ON THE OLD LOYALTIES
The Independent, October 1986

When Llanelli went to Old Deer Park to lose narrowly to London Welsh (a stirring event that went virtually unreported in the English Press), I noticed that they were up to their old tricks again. Or rather, their selectors had been up to them. Once more, players were being chosen out of position. A few weeks ago, when they played Harlequins – a match the west Wales side also just lost – the gifted Ieuan Evans was on the wing, while the almost equally gifted, but more subdued Kevin Thomas was proving a satisfactory replacement for the League-lost Gary Pearce at stand-off half.

At last, I thought, Thomas was restored to the position in which he had started out. The lad could look forward to some stability at least in this vale of tears. But no: last Saturday he had been switched to full-back. On Wednesday at Bristol he started as stand-off and finished at full-back again. Meanwhile, against London Welsh, Evans had more happily been moved to centre – the position he should surely occupy permanently.

Llanelli have a deplorable record of messing players about

to suit the club's convenience. Peter Hopkins began as a centre but now seems to have settled as a wing, in which position he is in and out of the side. Peter Morgan took years to fix himself at centre – though when he did he somehow failed to realise his earlier promise.

Obviously, from the nature of their trade, backs (excluding scrum-halves) can be shifted around more readily than forwards. But the latter can have their careers impeded as well. There was Roger Uttley. And Derek Quinnell did not gain as many caps as he ought to have done because neither club nor country could decide whether he was a lock, a No 8 or a blind-side flanker, the position in which he played so well for the 1971 Lions. The same pattern can be discerned in the career of Richard Moriarty of Swansea. It has presumably been decided not to play him at flanker any longer. But he is a No 8 for his club and a lock for his country. Yet the two positions are quite different. Even 35 years ago it was considered unsatisfactory for a forward such as Rees Stephens to oscillate between them. Today the game is more specialised still.

Nor is this self-created problem specifically Welsh. It is, however, seen in a particularly acute form in Wales, partly because the clubs play far too many hard matches which lead to injuries; partly because they can draw on a pool of young, versatile and, above all, ambitious backs, anxious to please their elders. One of those who took a firmer line was Gerald Davies. He decided that he was going to be a wing rather than a centre. No amount of cajoling by selectors would change his mind. But he was both an intelligent man and a great player.

An English player who now finds himself in a positional difficulty is Peter Williams of Orrell. Actually he is Welsh, or half-Welsh: his grandfather, Trevor Williams, was an outstanding forward for Ammanford, while his father Roy played for Llanelli, had a Welsh trial and then went north to Wigan, where he became Town Clerk. Anyway, for some months now the England selectors' plan has been to play Williams, usually a stand-off half, at full-back in the 1987 World Cup. This is quite a good wheeze, not least because – unusually, perhaps – the player concerned would welcome the change.

But he has suffered injuries, which cannot be helped. And he has not played regularly in his new position for his club. Indeed, Orrell have a perfectly good full-back in Simon Langford. It should not, however, be beyond the wit of the authorities to give Williams a little practice somewhere, if necessary by persuading him to change clubs. Likewise, if England are serious about playing Mark Bailey on the right wing, he should be there every Saturday, not on Wasps' left.

It is common to assert that all the old sporting virtues, including loyalty, are in decline. On the contrary: it seems to me that English, certainly London, players exhibit only too much loyalty to their clubs. It is wasteful that Wasps should possess two international full-backs and, even after the departure of Richard Cardus for Cardiff, three centres of international class. Two of these citizens should take themselves off to Richmond, Blackheath, Rosslyn Park or wherever. This would be preferable to playing the occasional match out of position or not playing at all.

LIGHT BLUES FADE BY DEGREES

The Independent, October 1986

Wilfred Wooller used to have a regular journalistic party piece, as he may still do. He would write that Oxford and Cambridge were now for swots only. Accordingly their rugby was of a lower standard than in days past. If current entrance requirements had been imposed in his day, he would go on, he would never have got into Cambridge at all.

I rather doubt this myself. The ancient universities still find ways of accommodating talented games players. Indeed, I suggested as much to my neighbour in the Press box when Richmond were playing Cambridge last Saturday. He represented a Cambridge paper. 'Don't tell me,' I said, 'that those chaps out there have got two As and a B at A-level, or two Bs and an A, or whatever it is they're asking for these days.' 'Some of them,' he replied courteously though with an air of correcting error, 'are brilliant, and have three As.' It would have been tempting to reply that they were certainly playing as if examinations were the only thing they were good at. But such a response would not only have been philistine – for there is no reason for rugby players not to be academically distinguished – it would also have been unfair. Everything considered, the university showed some promise – a minority view, I realise.

They were missing half their side, including Fran Clough. Mark Thomas was still sadly injured, nearly a year after the Steele-Bodger match. They were outweighted. It was a beastly cold afternoon with a strong wind. And yet Cambridge did some good things, being particularly quick on the break. Andy Cushing, the scrum-half, kept his head, and looked an altogether superior product to his opposite number from Richmond. Chris Oti, who played so well for Nottingham in last season's Middlesex Sevens, was faster than anyone the home side had on display, and scored a try on the one occasion he was given the ball.

There is no need to exaggerate. Some of the tackling was lamentable. This may well be the weakest Cambridge side for 15 years, as close observers were saying even before the match. Nevertheless, the interesting fact about the last couple of decades is surely not that university rugby has become so weak but that it remains so strong. In the mid-1960s most of the rugby commentators were writing that Oxford and Cambridge were of the past – that the future belonged to Loughborough and St Luke's. Well, it did not happen.

Logically, it ought to have happened. With the ending of National Service (which, while it continued, meant that undergraduates were two years older), then the more academically stringent entrance requirements and the abolition of many rugby-playing grammar schools, one would have expected university rugby to decline catastrophically.

Still, university rugby continues not perhaps to flourish as it once did –notably in the immediate post-war period – but certainly to prosper modestly. Consider some of the players produced recently. From Oxford we have Hugo MacNeill and now Brendan Mullin, Simon Halliday and Stuart Barnes.

From Cambridge we have an even more glittering collection of Rob Andrew, Mark Bailey, Simon Smith, Huw Davies, Kevin Simms, Fran Clough and Richard Moon.

One part of the explanation is that many of these players have not been 'produced' by Oxford or Cambridge at all. Thus MacNeill and Mullin were established Irish internationals before they went to Oxford. Davies was a product of the Cardiff Club and the Welsh Institute of Technology. Bailey came to Cambridge via Durham, as more recently did Oti. Cushing is quite a senior citizen who has played for London Scottish and is up at Cambridge as some kind of mature student. What seems to have happened is that the number of post-graduate students of one description or another has grown. The university rugby teams have benefited accordingly.

The other part of the explanation is that university players are good because, in England especially, they are given the chance to be good. I doubt whether Clough, for example, would be an England international today and in the current squad if he were an ordinary club player and not Simms's former partner at Cambridge. Favouritism, in short, still exists. The old universities benefit from that, too.

PHYSICAL JERKS IN A RUGBY DESERT
The Independent, November 1986

Phil Edmonds once told me that the reason he gave up playing rugby at Cambridge was Roger Michaelson, who, having previously captained the university, had returned as coach. Michaelson's idea was, as far as possible, to forget about the ball and instead to take the team on lengthy runs and arduous assault courses. This strenuous approach was not to Edmonds's taste. As he put it, if he had wanted to be a commando he would have joined the Royal Marines and not gone to Cambridge in the first place. As it was, he wished to enjoy himself playing rugby football but was not allowed to.

So he gave up the game (he had been a promising blind-side flanker or No 8).

In the subsequent decade and more, the Michaelson approach has triumphed. Fitness is all. We have read about Alan Jones, the Australian coach, telling Rob Andrew he was unfit and presenting him with a pair of running shoes. This week we have heard about the England squad's weekend in Portugal, variously described as interesting and knackering. It seems that Tom McNab, an expert on athletics and fitness generally, had the team doing sprints with their facial muscles relaxed. This is a notion of the great Dr Strabismus of Utrecht (whom God preserve). Indeed a good deal of rugby coaching now comes straight out of Beachcomber.

We should remember that fitness does not on its own put points on the board. It is not an end in itself. Let me make an analogy. A distinguished journalist was proudly showing me his recently-installed electronic equipment, screens, keyboards, that sort of thing. 'Marvellous machines,' I said. 'The only trouble is that you still have to think of the words, and get them in the right order.' Similarly with tries and goals. The England team may be as fit as McNab or anyone else likes. But, on the evidence of the Japanese match, the only basic skill which they have fully mastered is goal-kicking. And they have Marcus Rose to thank for that.

I used to assist a Cambridge full-back of a previous generation, Hugh Lloyd-Davies, with his goal-kicking practice. He was seven or eight years older than I was. My task was to stand behind the goalposts in the village of Tycroes, near Ammanford, and to retrieve the ball, scrambling it back to Lloyd-Davies as best I could. He would sometimes warm up by loping round the pitch in a perfunctory manner. This to him was 'training'. It was not, however, unproductive. Lloyd-Davies did after all win the university match of 1947 by kicking two penalties. And though he was not always the most reliable tackler or touch-finder, no one ever complained about his speed or stamina.

Goal-kicking can be practised in solitude – though my impression is that few current specialists do so, being kept too busy doing physical jerks. The England team's deficiencies are altogether less easy to remedy. What it comes down to is that they do not think fast enough or interestingly enough. It is not a trouble which afflicts the Irish, judged by their performance against Romania. When Michael Kiernan took the ball and transferred it in one movement, so bringing about a try, he reminded me not only of Philippe Sella but of an even finer French centre, Jo Maso.

Mick Doyle, the Irish coach, seems to have got the balance right between grimness and gaiety, fitness and flair. Gone is the time when the venerable Irish forwards, old soldiers like the members of Chiang Kai-shek's army, would find that their bootlaces required prolonged attention during the last quarter of the match. The team are fit enough. But they give the impression of enjoying their football, as the French have done for years and as the Australians now do.

Admittedly the Irish always enjoyed it too but in a different way, with the opponents' pass intercepted, the fly-kick chased or the ball hoisted high. Doyle has transformed them into a team both more formidable to play against and also more attractive to watch. By contrast, enjoyment is the feeling that seems to be lacking in the England team. Do not misunderstand me. Rugby cannot be enjoyed if you are gasping for breath or on the verge of collapse. But it cannot be enjoyed either if it is regarded as a sort of penance.

TIME TO SORT OUT A SPECIAL TV MESS
The Independent, November 1986

In the days when Brian Wenham was in charge of BBC2 (he has now bettered himself and become Controller of Radio) he and I, whenever we met, would have a short conversation as unchanging in form as any excerpt from the D'Oyly Carte Opera. 'When,' I would ask, 'are you going to broadcast *Rugby Special* at the same time on the same day, Sunday afternoon preferably?' Wenham, a rugby follower – which was why I was raising the matter – would look uneasy. 'I entirely agree it's got to be sorted out,' he would reply in placatory tones. 'But there are difficulties.'

This was the period when the programme would oscillate from month to month between Saturday and Sunday. On a Saturday evening many followers of the game were either on their way home from the match or having a drink somewhere. The programme now seems to have settled down on Sunday afternoon. But yet again the time varies. It started off the season at 1.35, and last week it had been moved to 2.05 – both awkward times also, when most people are having, preparing or drinking before lunch. You may think this a minor matter. On the contrary: regularity and predictability are not only as important as content but somewhat easier to put right.

Let me turn to content, however. Last Saturday France were playing New Zealand. It was the match every rugby follower wanted to see. Independent television secured the rights, and broadcast the game on Saturday afternoon in certain areas, including Wales – to the annoyance of the Welsh Rugby Union. It was scandalous that the BBC did not show it on *Rugby Special*. Instead, the programme showed Hawick and Gala. This was after a Saturday which had seen not only the French match but also Nottingham-Leicester, Bath-Wasps and Swansea-Llanelli. If there were difficulties about recording in Toulouse (though I see no reason for any), why did the Corporation not broadcast one of these attractive club fixtures?

A Scottish exile may object that Hawick-Gala is as interesting to a Border Scot as Swansea-Llanelli to a west Walian. I reply that there are numerous fixtures between Welsh clubs and those from London, the Midlands and the West Country. Supporters in England, even if they are not themselves Welsh, keep up with Welsh rugby as they do not with the Scottish or, for that matter, the Irish variety.

Virtually the sole advantage of showing Scottish matches on television is that it enables us to listen to Bill McLaren, one of the great masters of the commentating craft. I wish nevertheless that he would not predict so confidently that 'there will be rejoicing at Sudbury tonight' when someone from Wasps scores a try. Not on your life. In darkest Middlesex they will not be paying the slightest attention. Still, this is a quibble. Or, rather, it is a foible in him which is a cause of affection rather than an irritation – like the catchphrase of a venerable comedian. Though he tends to be something of an old dominie, too, which indeed he is by profession, we are lucky to have him.

Television commentating, even more than journalism, is an activity which almost everyone thinks he could successfully engage in if only given the chance. It is in fact very hard, as a comparison of McLaren with Nigel Starmer-Smith demonstrates. I have nothing against the latter, especially since he has escaped from his habit of talking about a 'ruck-situation' when he means a ruck. But quite apart from television scheduling and choice of match, Starmer-Smith's programme clearly leaves much to be desired.

Ian Robertson is the best rugby analyst since the late Carwyn James and is, moreover, on the BBC staff. But it is only rarely that we see him on the programme. The Welsh version of *Rugby Special* seems to provide a deeper analysis of the game and more peeps behind the scenes. Clearly this is not entirely Starmer-Smith's fault: presenters are front men, performers, who can do only as much as their producers allow. But equally clearly the programme is stuck in a groove.

DO NOT CHERISH THESE VILLAINS
The Independent, November 1986

Many years ago, when Her Majesty's judges really were judges – fierce, elderly parties, forever regretting that Parliament in its wisdom had deprived them of the power to order the prisoner to be flogged – there was a favourite judicial line when a criminal was accused of using a knife. The knife, they used to say, was a coward's weapon. Worse, it was unBritish. It was what the degenerate Latins employed to settle their frivolous disputes. The British way was to use your fists. A bare-knuckle fight was manly, even admirable.

If you substitute 'boot' for 'knife', you have the usually unspoken (but sometimes openly acknowledged) attitude towards violence in rugby held by many players, administrators and commentators. The boot is dangerous. You can seriously damage someone's brain or nervous system with a kick. A punch, by contrast, may be regrettable, but is usually delivered in anger and quickly forgotten. Moreover, in certain positions, the front row for instance, the odd blow is expected, part of the warp and woof of life. Steve Brain admitted as much in a recent newspaper interview. Nobody appeared scandalised or even mildly surprised. There was certainly no suggestion that Brain should be disciplined or persuaded to change his ways.

Similarly, in discussing David Bishop's case a commentator stated a few weeks ago that such episodes were common form. This, we may remember, was a case of a player's being hit by Bishop while he was held down by a member of Bishop's own side. Yet the writer concerned affected not to understand what the fuss was about. It went on all the time, he said. The only crime was to be caught.

Well, people are free to write what they like, more or less, subject to the law of libel and so forth – though such attempts at rugby sophistication and worldly wisdom do not greatly impress me, I confess. But rugby players are not, or should not be, free to do what they like.

Last Saturday Chris Mills, the Richmond prop, sustained a nasty eye injury from a punch delivered by Paul Moriarty, the Swansea flanker. A fortnight previously Stuart Russell, the London Welsh No 8, perhaps the most promising back row forward to have appeared in the past couple of seasons, suffered a detached retina, allegedly following a punch by an assailant from Moseley. It is fair to add that Moseley say the incident was not as simple as this. Russell had played only a few matches since his injury at the beginning of last season, and is understandably depressed.

Many of us who toddled to Old Deer Park to see Newport play London Welsh did so with a discreditable sense of pleasurable anticipation. We resembled rather the audiences that came to listen to Judy Garland. We thought something terrible might happen, and were unworthily excited at the prospect. In fact, nothing very terrible did happen. Mike Watkins, the Newport captain, confined himself largely to backchat with the referee Roger Quittenton, who is to Welshmen as Dr David Owen is to the Labour Party. They love to abuse the handsome fellow, but have a certain respect for him all the same. However, Jonathan Callard, the Newport centre, peppered punches on Jeremy Evans, the London Welsh flanker. The most culpable character on display was, I thought, Roger Powell, the Newport flanker.[1] And yet my heart went out to him in a way. He reminded me of some of the great villainous flankers of the past: Don White of Northampton, Ray Cale of Pontypool, Rory O'Connor of Aberavon and, most recently, Paul Ringer of Llanelli.

In a sense, we cherish our villains. But we should not do so. Nor should we place all the responsibility on the clubs. It is profitless to say they should not choose violent players, for they can and do choose them. It is only slightly less pointless for wronged clubs such as Richmond to insist that Swansea or whoever (generally a Welsh club) should themselves discipline erring players. The true responsibility lies with the home union concerned. A proper complaints procedure should be established operating a quasi-judicial system, with a hearing, representation (not necessarily by a barrister or solicitor), clearly-framed charges and due notice. We now operate a kind of lynch law instead.

[1] Mr Powell wrote courteously to me, denying any villainous intent, and I accepted his assurances.

THROW CAUTION TO THE WING
The Independent, December 1986

As Tuesday's university match went on, the cry could be heard even from Oxford supporters: 'Give it to Oti.' I had not witnessed such general agreement since the crowds at Cardiff Arms Park 40 years ago would shout: 'Give it to Bleddyn.' And, unlike the crowd at Twickenham, they were all supporting the same side.

As the game proceeded, it became manifest that whatever bright wheezes might be in the minds of the other Cambridge backs – notably Cushing, Lord, Wyles and Clough – giving the ball to this particularly dangerous wing was not among them. He received only two clean passes the whole match, from one of which he scored the sole try of the afternoon. There is nothing new or odd about such neglect. We should not single out Cambridge for blame. We have seen matches in which Rory Underwood did not receive a single pass.

The simple solution is to get the ball to the wing as quickly as possible, which the Australians have been doing for a long time. I have an additional suggestion, however. It is to play only one specialist wing, who would position himself on the open side, which would be on the right or the left as the case might be. The other wing could then be considered either as an additional full-back or as a blind-side wing. This modest proposal has its difficulties but is, I think, worth an experiment. It has, at any rate, a certain logic, given the way the game has been developing in the last 15 years or so.

Long ago wings came in all shapes and sizes, as they continue to do today. There were big, strong wings, medium-sized, stocky wings and little, nippy wings. But they had one thing in common. They spent most of their time standing around trying to keep warm. They were, nevertheless, certain to have the ball in their hands. This was because their solitary official duty was to throw the ball into the lineout. The opposing wing would stand at the front of the lineout, ready to tackle anyone who came up the touchline.

Then this comfortable arrangement changed. The French, oddly enough, were the last to persist with the old scheme, with wings of the highest class still throwing-in from touch using the underarm two-handed method, which was always rather despised in Britain. Under the new scheme, the hooker did the throwing-in. The blind-side wing retreated many yards from his traditional position, and was expected to function as an additional full-back. As wings play right and left, both of them are now expected to possess a full-back's skills.

It is in the nature of things that most of them do not have these abilities. There are, of course, exceptions, such as Mike Slemen. But most wings are traditional players who try to do their best at covering and kicking. It is surely preferable to play an additional full-back.

Several permutations are possible: right-back, left-back; wing, right centre, left centre. Then: open-side back, blind-side back; wing, right centre, left centre. Then: osb, bsb; w, outside centre, inside centre. And: rb, lb; w, oc, ic. As the wing is going to float, it is preferable to me to give the other players more fixed right-left positions, though there is still a case for a blind-side full-back. Either way, the English back division would then look something like this: M. Rose, H. Davies (or P. Williams); R. Underwood, J. Salmon, K. Simms (or S. Halliday); S. Barnes, R. Hill. And the Welsh back division: P. Thorburn , M. Dacey; G. Webbe, I. Evans, M. Ring (or B. Bowen or J. Devereux); J. Davies, R. Jones.

As the functions of the wing have changed so also have those of the full-back. Though there was the occasional tricky customer, the man of character was what was admired. He was expected to catch, kick and tackle, and it did not matter if he was not the fastest thing on two legs. The full-back is now an additional three-quarter. It makes sense to recognise this and to play only one wing, who will have twice the chance of getting his hands on the ball.

LAWS WHICH GO OVER THE TOP
The Independent, December 1986

At about this time last season, I remember, we were most of us saying that the new laws were working rather well, everything considered. There were fewer stoppages. The ball was being moved away from tackles and breakdowns more quickly than it had been a few years previously. And so forth.

Then the international championship started. It soon became evident not only that pile-ups were just as frequent, but also that referees were even more severe than they had been in fixing blame and awarding penalties. The kicker of goals was even more firmly seated behind his gun sights than ever. Philippe Sella apart, the dominating figures of the championship were all kickers: Gavin Hastings, Paul Thorburn and, to a lesser extent, Michael Kiernan and Rob Andrew. The only difference I can foresee in 1987 is that Marcus Rose, Stuart Barnes or both will replace Andrew in England's artillery. Nothing has really changed.

Certainly the referees have not changed. I never cease to be puzzled by the areas in which they will behave as indulgently as a fond father, and those in which they will descend on the luckless offender as heavily as the now-retired Mr Justice Melford Stevenson. For instance: forward passes currently tend to be ignored in the interests of open play if they are only a foot or so. It may be that we notice this laxity more than we used to on account of television and the near-vertical view it provides, enabling us to judge the path of the ball against the appropriate line.

Likewise, readjustments by the catcher are treated liberally. This is to be welcomed on the whole. But I am less happy about the ease with which tries are now awarded. The ball may be bobbing about behind the line. An attacker gets his hands on it and pats it down (sometimes forward, too) from some way off the ground. 'Try,' says the referee, raising his arm decisively. Yet the ball is still supposed to be grounded.

There is a luxury of further illustration. Backs encroach offside with impunity unless spotted by the referee, as they rarely are. And being additionally penalised for not retiring 10 yards after a penalty depends chiefly on whether an offender has been cheeking the ref in Mike Watkins style.

For other offences, however, referees don the black cap before they have even considered the evidence. There is now a fashion for regarding any high tackle whatever as dangerous. Thus Jamie Salmon was unjustly penalised in the Scottish match last season. In the same way, late tackles are invariably penalised, even when the offender was being impelled forward by his own momentum and inability to change course, rather than by any evil intent.

But the penalties which win and lose matches tend to come either from not releasing the ball or from going 'over the top'. I have always envied the confidence with which referees can judge that an 11-stone back submerged under several Japanese wrestlers such as Gareth Chilcott has 'failed to release the ball'. Usually there is nothing he would like to do more; unfortunately he cannot. 'Over the top' offences are perhaps less unjustly dealt with: but nevertheless an honest attempt to secure the ball can easily lead to three points for the other side.

I do not want to place all the blame on the referees as distinct from the laws – though they could still award more set scrums where they now give penalties. The truth is that the indirect free kick or differential penalty has been a failure. It is now awarded largely for accidental foot-up.

Even a crooked feed by the scrum-half is still penalised with a kick. Last Saturday Mark Douglas, of London Welsh, was, wrongly, penalised for this offence. The referee effectively gave Cardiff three points. The just course is to hand the ball to the opposing scrum-half. Why, after all, should a crooked feed be regarded as so much more heinous than a crooked throw into the lineout? This can be followed either by a throw from the other side or by a scrum. Most teams choose the latter.

I should like to see the laws modified to allow a choice for a wronged side between a scrum and a kick direct to touch – and to restrict kicks at goal to cases of foul, dangerous or deliberately unfair play. No such hope, I fear.

SQUADS STUCK IN THEIR OWN RIGIDITY
The Independent, January 1987

Rugby players as a class are probably more intelligent than a random sample of the population generally, though they often do their best to conceal it. Many players – even if not enough of the really top players – then go on to become administrators. Certainly the administrators, unlike those of other sports, almost always possess experience of some kind in the game they are meant to be regulating. Why is it, then, I often wonder, that officials get themselves into such a mess? As the *Daily Mail* likes to put it, why oh why? I muse along these lines about half a dozen times in a normal season; which is often enough.

The latest bout of melancholy reflection is occasioned by the English divisional 'trials', which were not trials in the proper sense because the national selectors were not allowed to choose the teams; by the on-off English trial tomorrow which was once thought to be off because Bath were being difficult; and by the Welsh trial which was supposed to be a fiasco because the Possibles not only beat the Probables but beat them decisively. I write 'supposed to' advisedly. For it is odd, when you come to think about it, to regard a trial as somehow unsuccessful if it disturbs preconceived notions and displays new prospects. What is a trial for, if not for these purposes?

In Wales the official response to the rise of, for instance, Glenn Webbe, Arthur Emyr, Mark Jones and Lyn Jones (who was not even given a trial) is more embarrassing than welcoming. Only the Llanelli players Ieuan Evans and, perhaps, the older Phil May – 'Thank God we've got our hands on a reliable second row at last' – seem to have been accommodated within the bounds of the selectors' thought.

The story is little different in England. Their selectors have stuck to the side, injured players apart, who performed so indifferently against Japan. The emergence of Jon Webb, Martin Offiah (not officially recognised yet), Chris Oti and Will Carling has been treated as ... well, as a bit awkward. Most inconvenient of all is the phoenix-from-the-ashes act of Richard Harding. He is, or ought to be, one of the game's immortals simply for knocking the ball out of Patrick Estève's palsied grasp at Twickenham two years ago. But he has always struck me as an underestimated scrum-half, in the shadow of a succession of inferior players well before the unlucky Nigel Melville and the peppery Richard Hill came on the scene.

The trouble lies in the squad system or, rather, in the abuse of the squad system (a point I owe to Clem Thomas). To begin with, the selectors form their squads too early in the season. They get ideas fixed in their heads which prove difficult to dislodge. Then, once the international championship is under way, they promptly destroy their squads – or, at any rate, the players' faith either in the squad or in the selectors.

Hardly a season goes by when, say, a left-wing does not drop out to be replaced by a right-wing. The most famous recent illustration is David Trick against Ireland. Or a No 8 is replaced by a lock who was not in the original squad at all; or a blind-side flanker by an open-side specialist who was not in the squad either but happened to make an impression on one of the selectors in a club match a few weeks previously.

The disadvantage of the squad system is its rigidity. This is also simultaneously its advantage: players know where they are and what is expected of them. You cannot have everything. But the time to introduce the rigidity – to form the squad and stick to the members – is after the selectors have looked at all the players, not before. Squads should last from January to April, not September to January.

SOUTH AFRICANS BEG THE QUESTION
The Independent, January 1987

The rugby championship of the world will be a splendid occasion. Everyone who is anyone will be there, together with numerous camp followers. We may even see some of the stirring events on television, though we can never be sure of these things with our capricious television authorities. It will not, however, be a true world championship. South Africa will not be participating. Whoever wins, the question will legitimately be asked: would they have beaten the South Africans?

Yet so far this has been a relatively quiet season as far as South African rugby's relationship to the rest of the world is concerned. Certainly it has been quiet if we consider recent happenings in the country itself and the international response to those events.

In England there have been several phantom teams flitting around the place. Rosslyn Park have played two South African internationals, and had a fixture with Wasps cancelled on their account. The Park coach who was partly responsible for bringing these individuals into the team, David Barclay, has resigned – though we are told he was going to resign anyway. The Richmond coach, Derek Wyatt, takes the opposite approach. He is said to be at odds with some people in the club on that account.

At the very end of last season, however, five leading South African players – D. M. Gerber, S. W. P. Burger, C. J. du Plessis, H. E. Botha and P. R. van der Merwe – appeared in the celebratory matches at Cardiff and Twickenham. Oddly enough, there was hardly a demonstrator in sight or even an eyebrow raised. For myself, I was glad to see them. This modest satisfaction was not shared generally by what are sometimes misleadingly called liberals. The liberal line on sporting connections with South Africa has shifted in several important respects in the past few years.

The modern line (which, I emphasise, is not confined to the hard left) is that South Africans are to be shunned and avoided, barred and excluded, simply because of the country they come from, irrespective of their race, colour or political views. While Mrs Winnie Mandela might be welcome, a team from South Africa of mixed race and colour would be prohibited. The prohibition would usually be enforced (maybe illegally) by a local authority, refusing to grant permission to use a ground.

The other respect in which the liberal line has shifted is that formerly it was said that there was no evidence that playing rugby against South Africa did anything to change political attitudes there. On the contrary: it still remained a cruel and miserable country. Playing rugby merely strengthened the cause of the ruling party, for that party's game was not only oppression but rugby also.

I used to be – still am – sympathetic to this argument.

Playing rugby against South Africa was different from playing against Romania, say. It was different because the Communist (indeed Stalinist) government of Romania did not attach nearly so much importance to the game as a symbol both of nationhood and of acceptance. It was different also because there was a political or, if you prefer, moral distinction between a totalitarian government which oppressed all its citizens and a racialist government which oppressed those of its citizens who had dark skins, or whatever the lunatic criteria happened to be. The former kind of government was and is less bad than the latter.

But today the liberal argument is changed. It is now that no good can come about in South Africa, and no good can come out of it, in any circumstances whatever, short of revolution. There is nothing else to be done. In other words, the South African government could produce evidence – though I am not saying it has yet satisfactorily produced such evidence – that it was operating a multi-racial policy in rugby. This would be no use. It could additionally welcome a team containing, for instance, Chris Oti and numerous other black players, assuring them of its highest regard. This would be no use either.

Just as I am against persecuting or discriminating against individual players simply because they are South African, so also am I against refusing to countenance any evidence whatever that the country has changed for the better. If it could show that evidence, I should welcome South Africa at the rugby championship of the world.

A SILLY SEASON FIT FOR HEROES
The Independent, January 1987

The modern world is so arranged that we seem able to recognise and accept only one hero or heroine at a time. This is particularly true of sport. It is most markedly true of rugby. I do not propose to read another article about, or interview with, Jonathan Davies until the season is over.

This is not because the papers contrive to spell his places of birth and residence wrongly (respectively Trimsaran and Cefneithin) but, rather, because the entire Jonathan Davies phenomenon has got quite out of hand. Thus: he is not only the best stand-off half currently operating in Europe, which is a perfectly reasonable statement to make. More than this: he is the best in the world. He is the best, further, who has ever played for Wales. He is probably the best in the entire history of the game, anywhere in the world.

This kind of talk is silly. Sportsmen (with the exception, perhaps, of athletes and a few others) cannot be judged apart from their own eras, because rules and conditions change so much. I wish Davies well, in League as much as in Union. But just as one player may be exalted – for a time – so are others dropped, depreciated, forgotten and, sometimes, rehabilitated.

Paul Simpson of Bath is an example of this final category. He last played for England three years ago against Scotland, in the equivalent of the match that was to have taken place tomorrow. Shortly before that, in 1983, he had played his first international, against New Zealand at Twickenham. His performance was generally agreed to have been the outstanding one among the forwards on either side. Then, all of a sudden, poor Simpson was out of favour. He was supposed to be too short. He spent either too much or too little of his time on the floor (for the moment, I forget which). He was a No 8 for his club, and so could not be a flanker for his country. And so forth.

Now, you cannot be the outstanding forward on the field against New Zealand and yet not good enough a couple of months later. It does not make sense. Simpson, however, is one of the lucky minority, being given a chance again. Others are more harshly treated. Simon Smith of Wasps is one example that comes to mind. His club have now restored him to his regular position on the right wing. For a time he had the experience (whether mortifying or not I do not know) of being switched with Mark Bailey in order to accommodate the national selectors' plans for Bailey.

They have now jettisoned Bailey and replaced him not with

Smith but with Mike Harrison of Wakefield. Harrison is a good player. So is Bailey. But Smith never once let England down, any more than did his predecessor John Carleton. We can all think of similar injustices in the other national sides which, if they were perpetrated by an employer, would lead to large sums being awarded in damages by an industrial tribunal.

In Wales there was no reason to drop Alan Phillips of Cardiff five years ago in favour of Billy James of Aberavon. Now James has been replaced not by Alan but by another Phillips, Kevin, of Neath. He in turn supplanted Mike Richards both at his club and from national contention. Form can vary, true, but it does not vary as much as all that. Playing styles can be changed by coaches. But a good player remains a good player.

Last season, for instance, there was a lot of exaggerated talk about John Jeffrey of Kelso. 'They call him the White Shark.' No, they don't call him anything of the kind, but he was and is an outstanding flanker. And yet this season Jeffrey's position was supposed to be in doubt. As in Simpson's case, it does not entirely add up.

Still less does the history of Tony Ward, of several Irish clubs. In the last six years he has played only three times for Ireland, on one of these occasions as a replacement. Here, political – I mean rugby-political – considerations seem to have been operating, quite apart from his justified replacement by Ollie Campbell. One version is that he annoyed the selectors by posing, scantily attired, for a photograph in one of our great popular newspapers. Ward might still recoup substantial damages from our rugby industrial tribunal in the sky.

PLAYING UP THE ACTIVE SUPPORT ROLE
The Independent, January 1987

The late J. P. W. Mallalieu was once asked on an *Any Questions?* programme whether it would not be a good thing for more people to participate in sport rather than merely to watch it. The other panellists on the show had been making conventional noises about health, fitness, participation and the rest of it. Nonsense, said Mallalieu. There was no 'merely' about supporting a team. It was an active occupation – what is now called, in the horrible jargon of 1987, 'positive'. He could speak with some authority, for he was not only a Huddersfield Town supporter but also one of the two Labour MPs since the war to win a rugby Blue (the other was Richard Stokes).

He was speaking at a time before soccer violence and, indeed, the hooliganism which is now developing in one-day cricket. Significantly, this cricket hooliganism is confined largely to Somerset supporters. It is significant because, in rugby, Bath – closely rivalled in this respect by Gloucester – have the nastiest, most objectionable supporters in England or Wales. Is this because there is no longer a first class soccer team in the West Country that the youth of the region can follow?

This is not, I may say, metropolitan fastidiousness on my part. The supporters of the Welsh clubs are men of peace who argue with and sometimes abuse the referee (always, if he is Roger Quittenton) only because they feel it is expected of them. Leicester supporters never give any trouble and satisfy their instincts by dressing themselves up like Christmas trees in red, white and green. The London Irish crowd, however, are the best of the lot: wittier, better humoured and more hospitable than the Welsh, and equally scholarly in their approach and nice in their discriminations. The Wasps crowd are very friendly. I should put them second to the Irish.

The Harlequin supporters (members rather) are mostly all right, once you get to know them, but they are expected to wear their technicoloured ties at matches, which is silly. What is even sillier is that they are further prohibited from wearing these club ties on any other occasion. What is the point of buying a tie if you can put it on only once a week? This is the kind of made-up boys' school rule which makes some of us think that the English are quite off their heads.

The Richmond members are even more prone to get themselves up like dummies in Burtons window *circa* 1955, sporting not only striped club ties but double-breasted navy blue blazers and cavalry twill trousers with turn-ups, though these last may now be back in fashion for all I know. London Scottish, who share a ground and clubhouse with Richmond, tend to be more adventurous and various in their attire. Of Blackheath, Rosslyn Park and Saracens I cannot speak with authority, not having been to their grounds very often.

From all of which you will nevertheless rightly conclude that I am a watcher, a mover around, rather than a natural supporter of any one team. This was so long before I began to write about the game. When I was a boy my father would take me to see Swansea or Llanelli, depending on which side were playing at home and whether the fixture was sufficiently attractive.

For the last 25-odd years, ever since I ceased working on Saturdays, I have traversed London but with a strong inclination towards the Richmond and Twickenham areas, in particular Old Deer Park. After the match, however, we do not go for a drink to the main clubhouse but to the Mid-Surrey Bowls Club, which also has premises on the ground. A few years ago a friend of mine, a fully paid-up member, tried to buy a drink in the London Welsh clubhouse and was refused, being told from a great height that he was at a bar that was reserved for members of the committee and their guests. Whereupon he pronounced that this was 'contrary to the spirit of Rugby Union football' – whatever that may be exactly – and took us all off to the Bowls Club instead. We have gone there ever since. Neil Kinnock followed us in due course.

QUESTION OF TASTE QUOTING THE DEAD
The Independent, January 1987

A few weeks ago I quoted the late Ricky Bartlett in this column and received an irate letter from a member of the Harlequins club as a result. (If you want to be pedantic, they call themselves the Harlequin Football Club, without the little 's', or any mention of rugby either: but this is by the way.) It was intolerable, this gentleman asserted, to quote someone when he was dead. Not only was it in bad taste. The person quoted was in no position to issue a denial.

The strict application of this principle would instantly expunge most of contemporary history from the books. I remain uncontrite. Though I never, I hope, go out of my way to cause offence, I shall have to bear the disapproval of the man from the Quins with such fortitude and equanimity as I can summon. I go on to quote Bartlett again. He said that, if he were a young man today, he would no longer be prepared to play first class rugby, such were the pressures and the demands. He went on to say that, in his opinion, some form of part-time professionalism in Rugby Union, on League lines, was both inevitable and desirable.

I am fairly sure that, if Bartlett had been young now, he would indeed be playing first class rugby. He might make fun of the coaches. He might skip training and be dropped temporarily as a consequence, 'as a disciplinary measure', as they say. He would certainly have no part in the 'psyching-up' procedures which are common form today. It is difficult to imagine old Ricky yelling: 'What are we going to do?'; more difficult still to imagine him shouting in reply: 'We're going to win.' Yet such was his love for the game that he would still have played it. He turned out for Sunday rugby in Surrey when he was well into his 50s.

But his prediction about the inevitability of part-time professionalism remains valid. All institutions change by pretending that they are doing nothing of the kind but instead extending existing practices. That is the way in which changes are commonly brought about.

The most interesting development of the season so far is the agreement of the French and Welsh Rugby Unions to support payment for 'broken-time', in particular for wages lost by players while undertaking overseas tours. 'Broken-time' was, as we know, the question over which the League split from the Union, even though it was money lost while playing in this country (as distinct from abroad) that was at issue. I would advise the unions concerned to jettison this incandescent phrase, redolent as it is of past controversies, and to think up another one.

Again, as I write, I have before me a communication from the Rugby Football Union. It has, I learn, great pleasure in inviting me to a reception to announce the sponsorship of the English Clubs Rugby Union Championship, to be held on 9 February at the West Pavilion Suite, Twickenham, at 11.30 a.m. for 12 noon. I am asked to reply to Mike Coley, Marketing Manager, Rugby Football Union. No doubt it will be a delightful social occasion, even if a trifle early in the day for someone of my industrious habits. But what, I should like to know, is the Rugby Union doing with a marketing manager at all? What is it precisely that he is meant to be marketing? We all know the answer. Mr Coley is there to obtain money from commercial organisations which is then, as the phrase goes, channelled back into the game.

Several factors have operated to bring about this state of affairs: Britain's brief period of international pre-eminence in the early 1970s; the consequential, or anyway contemporaneous, rise of rugby as a televised sport; and the emergence of commercial sponsorship in sport generally. Rugby, in short, is being used as an arm of advertising and public relations. Nothing wrong in that, as such. But can a sport logically or reasonably be professional at the one end and amateur at the other? It is surely a standard case of the left hand's not knowing what the right hand is up to.

When Glenda Jackson appears in a television commercial for Hanson Trust she adds to her much-admired collection of fine old English banknotes, and doubtless satisfies her socialist conscience simultaneously. It is up to her, one person. The game of rugby is composed of many persons, of whom the most important are the players. They should surely benefit too.

ODDS-ON FOR THE DRAW BANKER

The Independent, February 1987

I have a friend who, for the past few seasons, has put £10 on a draw for every match in the international championship. There is, as we were most of us told in our youth – and have almost certainly discovered since for ourselves – no infallible system for making money from betting. But he says his method is one of the best he knows.

The reasoning is as follows: there are 10 matches in the championship. Total investment, £100. The odds against a draw vary between 12-1 and 16-1 depending on the match and the bookmaker, with 14-1 as the average price (not just the arithmetical average but the price which, season after season, is quoted most frequently by far). One draw, one only, means you are in profit for the season. Two draws and you are buying champagne for your friends. Three, and you can go away for the weekend. There were no draws last season, but two the season before that. So my friend is still in profit over the past two years.

As we know, it is all fun, not *sérieux* to a proper betting man, which I am not. Ron Pollard, who seems to combine the functions of old-fashioned bookmaker and modern public relations officer, told me years ago that Ladbrokes went in for betting on politics as a form of free advertising or loss-leader. The money taken was a tiny proportion of the turnover from other forms of gambling. Rugby is rather similar in this respect. Ladbrokes expect to take £30,000 on the international championship compared to £5 million on the Derby alone.

Let us, however, have a look at the prices which Ladbrokes are offering (the other big bookmakers may vary slightly): France 8-11, Scotland 7-2, Ireland 6-1, Wales 8-1 and England 10-1. This amounts to a prediction by the bookmakers of both the outcome of the championship and the weight of money that will fall on the five countries. The object is, of course, to make a profit whatever happens.

I think France will win the championship, but the odds

offered are not at all attractive, even if we allow for the rearranged season. A lot can happen between now and the beginning of April. Risking £10 for a speculative gain of £7.27 does not sound much fun.

One cannot really complain, I suppose, about Scotland's being made second favourites, even if a long way after France. But I think the bookmakers, their hard-headedness notwithstanding, have been over-influenced by last season, when the Scots shared the championship with the French.

The English price, by contrast, seems attractive. I would not invest any money in them myself but some native-born sentimentalists might like to.

I am certainly not sentimental about Wales. During this decade the championship has been won by these countries: Ireland, three times; France, three; Scotland, two; and England, one. France, however, have won the championship outright only once, sharing it in 1983 and 1986 with Ireland and Scotland respectively. Ireland, on the other hand, have won it twice outright. Accordingly, Ireland must in justice be nominated the team of the 1980s thus far, with Wales nowhere. Surely, my compatriots say, Wales's turn must come, come soon. How long, Oh Lord, how long!

It is a bit like the arguments we used to have before the examinations. One of the consolations of middle age is that such disputes will never recur. A certain topic – the War of the Spanish Succession, say – has not come up for six years. Bound to come up this year, obvious. Alas, there is again no question on the War of the Spanish Succession.

Likewise with Wales. They never seem to come up – partly because the selectors insist on choosing an inadequate set of back five forwards. This is a piece of perversity which persists with the omission of Phil May, Mark Jones and Lyn Jones. My modest tenner will be going on Ireland. I may be influenced by having won with them two years ago, when they were 8-1.

There are broadly two views about betting. One is that you decide who are going to win, and put as much money as you can afford on them, irrespective of the odds. The other is that you take the odds into account from the beginning, and decide which is the most attractive bet. I am of the second school, thinking that France will win but that Ireland at 6-1 are the best bet.

ABUSING THE GIFT OF FREE SPEECH

The Independent, February 1987

It was during the equivalent French match 20 years ago that the Twickenham crowd first started to shout for England. Previously, they had been more restrained. Though recollections may differ, and memory is tricky, it was around this time that the chant of 'England, Eng-land' became current. What is certain is that this period immediately followed England's victory in the soccer World Cup of 1966. It was in Harold Wilson's rather than in Margaret Thatcher's Britain that the Union Jack became a popular symbol, not only waved at football matches, but used as a decorative motif for coffee mugs and the like.

The volume of English rugby support has remained roughly constant in the succeeding 20-odd years, if anything diminishing slightly. Whether the team would play better if the crowd shouted louder is doubtful: my guess is that it would not make much difference. Players seem to be conscious only of a general level of noise, irrespective of its source, and also of the quick passage of time: they are surprised when the match is over so soon. Even goal-kickers do not appear to be put off by booing.

I mention this not to defend the practice but because I received several letters bringing it up after my observations on the behaviour of crowds a few weeks ago. How dare I – so the argument ran – criticise the behaviour of West Country crowds when Welsh crowds were so free with their boos. Well, attacking the former does not necessarily entail defending the latter: but booing is a difficult subject nonetheless.

One view is that it is a nasty, unpleasant noise which is not justified in any circumstances whatever. You might call this the television commentator's approach, or McLaren's Morality. But there are occasions, I think, when spectators are entitled to express their feelings in this way. Such behaviour is different from the sadly increasing practice of booing at the theatre or the opera. Here the performers have done their best and any disapproval should be directed at the producer or director, who is unseen. In rugby, the spectator is booing a decision of the referee with which he disagrees, or an action by a player which he deplores. Booing a place-kicker is a different matter, however little he may be put off.

Booing during the playing of national anthems is regrettable – though there was perfunctory booing during 'God Save the Queen' at Cardiff a few seasons ago because, in a representative as distinct from an international match, the Welsh national anthem was not played at all. In short, my bias is towards free speech for spectators. It can, however, be abused, as we are told often enough these days in different connections.

There used to be a London Welsh supporter at Old Deer Park who specialised in being scathing at the expense of the visiting team. He looked rather like the German novelist Gunter Grass, with a drooping moustache, and he would stand behind the goalposts. Last season, Bath were unexpectedly behind, and Welsh had just scored another try. As the visiting players were retreating behind their line for the conversion attempt, Roger Spurrell, the then Bath captain, confessed that he found the state of affairs 'bloody incredible', as well he might.

He then received some abuse from the supporter with the moustache. Spurrell began to walk towards his tormentor. 'Carry on talking,' he said, now about six feet away. The Welsh supporter had, however, clearly decided that silence was the more prudent course. Spurrell stood facing him, hands on hips. The rest of us wondered what would happen next, and what, if anything, we ought to do should the worst occur. At that moment the conversion went over, the Bath linesman shouted 'Come away, Roger,' and away Roger duly went to engage in the rest of the game. He left in his wake a quaking, chastened Welsh supporter who has yet to recover the use of his voice.

There is no doubt that, week after week, this particular supporter went too far. Sometimes his interjections could be quite funny, but more often they were merely abusive. And yet, are players entitled to respond to abuse with threatening behaviour? I do not think so. Perhaps the chairman of Bath rugby club would like to write another letter to the paper on this subject.

THIS IS WHAT THE GAME IS ALL ABOUT
The Independent, February 1987[1]

'Good afternoon, Bill.'

'Good afternoon, Nigel.'

'Well, here we are at the Cardiff Arms Park or rather, I should say, the National Stadium. What was it called in your playing days, Bill?'

'It's interesting you should ask me that, Nigel, because, blow me, it's so long ago I can't remember.'

'Ha, ha.'

'But what I do remember is that after 80 minutes out there you knew you'd been in a match and no mistake.'

'It's certainly a veritable cauldron of emotion still. Anyway here is Jonathan Davies, the brilliant young Neath stand-off half, whom many shrewd observers have compared to the late Barry John, with the kick off. He's following the modern fashion and booting it over the dead ball line. Any comments on that, Bill?'

'That's an interesting point, Nigel, because England have to drop out and concede possession and territorial advantage. But I think you can overdo these new-fangled notions.'

'Thank you, Bill. The England forwards are certainly piling in. They want to show that their inspiring performance against the French at Twickenham two weeks ago was no flash in the pan. As you will be able to see when the camera gets round, there are already three Welsh forwards flat on their backs.'

'England, have served notice, Nigel, that they're not going to be messed around by anyone.'

'As the old Duke of Wellington put it, they're getting their retaliation in first.'

'I always thought it was Field Marshal Montgomery, Nigel, before the battle of Alamein, but we won't argue about that.'

'Certainly not when Gareth Chilcott, the uncompromising Bath prop, has been laid out, or so it seems, in an unprovoked assault by Stuart Evans, the uncompromising Neath prop. Clearly a penalty, Bill.'

'I agree, Nigel. Marcus Rose has kicked more penalties at this distance than I've had hot dinners.'

'And he's done it. Any advice to England at this stage, Bill?'

'Richard Hill should be saying: Look, lads, cool it a bit. Settle down. Let's get the ball off the park, safe in touch. Then hopefully Marcus Rose will be able to slot some more penalties.'

'It looks as if Hill isn't taking your advice, Bill. He's actually running with the ball and he's giving it to Ieuan Evans. Is Evans offside, Bill? Anyway no one's going to stop him now. Chilcott, the only man in pursuit, will never catch him from this distance.'

'A very lucky score, Nigel. I think that Ieuan Evans was morally offside although the laws don't agree with me. And what made it more unfair still was that Rory Underwood, the RAF flyer, who would have given the gifted young Llanelli three-quarter a run for his money, was stuck on the other side of the field.'

'It would have been against the run of play if that conversion had gone over. As it is, England can still salvage this match. And a penalty. What was that for, Bill?'

'I'm fairly sure it was for dangerous play by Stuart Evans, the uncompromising young Neath prop, Nigel.'

'This should present Marcus Rose with no difficulty. And the Harlequins and former Cambridge University full-back, restored to favour after six years in the wilderness, has done it again. Any advice to England in the second half, Bill?'

'I think Richard Hill should be saying to the lads: Look, lads, let's control the pace of this match. Settle down a bit. Get the ball off the park out of harm's way, that's what this game of rugby's all about.'

'Thank you, Bill. In the meantime, a ruck-situation has developed just outside the English 22-metre line. Jonathan Davies seems to have dropped a goal. The referee certainly appears to think so because he's pointing at the centre spot.'

'It wasn't one of young Jonathan's better efforts, Nigel. That ball lurched through those posts as if it would fail the breathalyser, no trouble.'

'My own feeling was that it was a straight toe punt by the gifted young Welsh half-back. But England have everything to play for still. Oh, a penalty to England, thank goodness, I mean thoroughly justified. What was it for, Bill?'

'Some nonsense between Stuart Evans and Gareth Chilcott, Nigel. Marcus Rose should have no difficulty.'

'Well done, Marcus. And there goes the final whistle with English pride restored. They didn't score any tries but it's what's on the board that counts. Many congratulations to Martin Green, who's taken a lot of stick and who's restored English pride.'

'Good afternoon, Nigel.'

'Good afternoon, Bill.'

---

[1] Written before the notorious encounter at Cardiff between England and Wales.

PITCHING IN TO GIVE WINTER RELIEF
The Independent, April 1987

The international matches that are being played tomorrow are something of a bonus. The championship would have ended a fortnight ago if the season had gone according to plan. But we had snow in January, which took us all by surprise – bless my soul, snow in January – and the games had to be put off. The Twickenham authorities were insistent that the pitch was, or would have turned out to be, fit for play. They postponed the match because spectators and players, particularly Scottish players, would have found difficulty in reaching the ground. This was certainly the right decision.

But should the authorities have been placed in the position of having to make the decision at all? There is a case for not playing any rugby whatever in January or in both January and February. In the north of Scotland they have a rest from rugby in mid-season. On the European continent they give up soccer in January and February. Soccer in this country is run by unimaginative men. Rugby administrators would not, I grant you, be many lengths ahead in the imagination stakes. But they are not subject to the same pressures to make profits bulge or, as is more usual, ends meet.

Nor would the players, I think, object to a break. I was at Sudbury on 10 January when Wasps were playing Llanelli, the pitch was visibly freezing, and the snows were about to descend. The referee stopped the match after 10 minutes of the second half. The wonder was that the game went on in the first place – and that the players performed so well.

As Tommy Bedford, the great South African No 8, once asked, when he was in this country at Oxford University: 'Why do they have to play when it's so cold?' His solution was to extend the season into May and June. This new arrangement would inevitably affect players who also played cricket. The elongation of the football season has meant the elimination of the old-style, year-round, double professional, of whom the most famous example was perhaps Denis Compton. But the increasing professionalisation of cricket has meant also that rugby players do not find places in county sides as readily as they once did.

Let us, however, assume that a period of total rest from rugby at the beginning of the year is too radical even for Mrs Thatcher's Britain. That still leaves the international season to consider. A total of 10 matches are now played in five groups of two, at intervals of a fortnight. This is the arrangement which satisfies the countries, the clubs and the BBC. We could maintain it and have the season extending from the middle of February to the end of April instead of, as at present, the beginning of January to the middle-to-end of March. Or we could have weekly internationals, one every

Saturday, on the same mid-February to end-of-April timetable.

My own preference, I confess, would be for an end-of-season spectacle, with two internationals being played on five successive Saturdays, ending on the last Saturday in April. The John Player and Schweppes Cups would be unaffected, except that the semi-finals would have to be out of the way before the start of the short but intense international season.

There is a separate but connected matter which I should also like to bring up: the state of first class pitches. You are more likely to have fine, dry weather in April than in January, but the ground will have more worn patches in the later months.

The short point is that all season round the condition of many pitches is a scandal. My colleague Tim Glover rightly wrote on Monday that the condition of the Wasps pitch for the semi-final against Leicester was a disgrace – to say nothing of the muddy surrounds through which spectators had to pick their way. He suggested that the John Player semi-finals should be played on neutral grounds, as the Schweppes semi-finals are.

There is a strong case for this on the basis of equity, but a less strong case on the basis of playing conditions. The neutral pitch might, after all, be in an even worse state than the home pitch. Even the National Ground was in a shocking condition for the England-Wales match. Pitches do not get up and hit people. But they are a principal part of the messy conditions in which people are likely to be hit.

THE LIONS WHO STILL LOOK LIKE THE LOSERS

The Independent, April 1987

The fact that the various countries are sending national teams to the World Cup should not prevent us from engaging in the traditional pastime of rugby followers at this time of year: picking the Lions.

Before the season started, my order was: Ireland, Scotland, Wales and England. As the championship progressed, Scotland moved into the domestic lead, but after last Saturday's stirring events matters look different.

Still, Gavin Hastings has done enough to make himself the first-choice full-back. Marcus Rose has had a marvellous season, but it is easy to see why he is not – how can one put it? – the most popular of players. On being asked a straightforward, standard, daft question on *Rugby Special* last Sunday, he really had no business saying the equivalent of 'Hello, mum' to the players dropped after the Welsh match. Hugo MacNeill always looks more impressive playing for Ireland than for London Irish. But I should settle for Paul Thorburn as Hastings's No 2, even though we have not seen a lot of him this season.

The outstanding right-wing is Trevor Ringland, though he finds difficulty both in catching and in hanging on to the ball. Mike Harrison would be my reserve.

Rory Underwood is still more of a promise than a performance, admittedly through no fault of his own. He must still, however, be the first choice on the left. As his reserve I should follow Lions tradition and bring in an uncapped player, either Chris Oti or Arthur Emyr who, scandalously, is not even in the recently-announced Welsh squad.

My first-choice centres would be Jamie Salmon and Brendan Mullin, both of whom had good seasons. Far from needing four centres in a squad of 26, as the Welsh absurdly imagine, you do not need as many as four specialists in a squad of 30. I should include either Malcolm Dacey or Huw Davies or even both of them as utility players. If only one were taken, I should include Michael Kiernan, both for his goal-kicking and for his ability to play on the wing.

Before last Saturday there were good judges who would have preferred John Rutherford and Roy Laidlaw as the half-backs. No longer: Jonathan Davies and Robert Jones are restored to the top, even though Wales lost. Michael Bradley, Richard Harding or both would almost certainly have to be flown out owing to injury as the tour progressed.

The tight-heads choose themselves, Iain Milne and Stuart Evans, with the latter as my first choice on account of his slightly greater mobility. There should also be no argument about David Sole at loose-head. There is a shortage of outstanding reserves: Jeff Whitefoot is not the force he was, and Paul Rendall last Saturday stood up better to Milne. I should take Rendall, just.

Colin Deans would be hooker and captain, while it does not really matter who goes as his reserve. I should go for Alan (rather than Kevin) Phillips, partly to show the Welsh selectors what I thought of them.

At lock it is back to the old firm of Donal Lenihan and Robert Norster. Steve Bainbridge must certainly go too, and his partner would be Nigel Redman or Willie Anderson, with a slight preference for Anderson on account of his versatility.

In the back row we are overwhelmed by a luxury of talent. None of it is Welsh. John Beattie is first choice No 8. I should settle for Dean Richards as Beattie's reserve on the strength of his muscular performance last Saturday.

The two blind-side flankers choose themselves, Paul Matthews and John Jeffrey, with Matthews as first choice. The open side is the hardest of all to fill – or the easiest, if you look at it differently, for there are so many good players. Once again I should go for a discard, Peter Winterbottom, despite Gary Rees's endeavours against Scotland; partly because Winterbottom is one of the few British players envied in New Zealand. I should take Nigel Carr as his reserve, though Finlay Calder could just consider himself hard done by.

The Test team: G. Hastings (Scotland); T. Ringland (Ireland), J. Salmon (England), B. Mullin (Ireland), R. Underwood (England); J. Davies (Wales), R. Jones (Wales): D. Sole (Scotland), C. Deans (Scotland, capt), S. Evans (Wales), D. Lenihan (Ireland), R. Norster (Wales), P. Matthews (Ireland), J. Beattie (Scotland), P. Winterbottom (England).

Would they beat New Zealand, Australia or France? No, but that is not my fault.

THE TIME TO HAND OUT THE BOUQUETS

The Independent, April 1987

This is the time to distribute prizes and anti-prizes. It is not, however, an exercise to be taken over-seriously.

Club of the season: Bath, alas. When André Gide was asked to nominate the best French poet he replied: Victor Hugo, alas. Likewise with Bath. They are now a bit like Arsenal in the 1930s. They win everything, but nobody really loves them very much.

Everybody likes Wasps, the West Ham United of rugby. I shall be cheering them inwardly at Twickenham in eight days' time (for we are expected to behave ourselves in the Press box. Here, by the way, is a curious difference: music critics applaud performances they are writing about, whereas rugby and political correspondents alike are supposed to keep quiet.) Runners-up: Neath. Commendations: Nottingham and Orrell.

Club on the slide, though there were special circumstances this season: Barbarians. It is, however, a sign of something or other when the Stanley and Steele-Bodger XVs to meet Oxford and Cambridge respectively are stronger than the Barbarian teams to meet Cardiff and Swansea. My solution (though it is not original) is to have the British Lions play as a touring club.

Player of the season: tie between the two Erics, Champ and Bonneval of France. Runner-up: Mike Harrison of Wakefield. Most exciting players: Chris Oti of Nottingham and Martin Offiah of Rosslyn Park. Most underestimated player: Steve Bates of Wasps. Unluckiest player: Lyn Jones of Neath.

Luckiest player: tie between Richard Hill, Graham Dawe and Gareth Chilcott of Bath, all of whom were restored to the England squad largely for reasons of sentiment and team morale. Wade Dooley of Fylde is different, for there is a case for restoring him on playing grounds, though I should have taken Maurice Colclough of Swansea instead, despite his advancing years.

National team of the season: France, obviously. Runners-up: Scotland, despite their sad performance in the west London drizzle. This match against England showed, among other things, that you cannot have two wings playing as centres, even though Keith Robertson has some experience as the latter: the more so if both players are, by modern standards, small men.

I do not reproach Mick Doyle and his team for losing me £10. At 7-1 it was a good bet.

The English higher command, Mike Weston and Martin Green, were as muddle-headed as ever, even after their final success: on the one hand saying that they wanted to enjoy themselves, and, on the other hand, maintaining an atmosphere of Cromwellian puritanism and austerity.

The booby prize, however, goes unhesitatingly to Rod Morgan and friends. I dealt with them last week, and no more need be said at this juncture, though I shall doubtless be returning to the subject in the future.

County of the season: Yorkshire, and not just for winning the county championship. In winning they played some of the most attractive rugby seen at Twickenham this season, with Rob Andrew showing that he can still make a break when he wants to. The Twickenham authorities ran out of programmes 40 minutes before the kick off; typical, I am afraid.

Farce of the season: the merit tables. Matches were demeritised, if that is the correct word, on the unilateral decision of one of the clubs when such a course seemed convenient, even though the clubs specifically undertook not to behave in this way when the tables were inaugurated. Next season we have a new system, which I await without too much hope.

Most promising development of the season: the greater freedom of movement between Rugby Union and amateur Rugby League. For example, there are now Oxford and Cambridge Rugby League sides. Some of the players are Union Blues. Labour MPs such as Roger Stott of Wigan and Merlyn Rees of Leeds both think that much remains to be done to bring the two codes closer together. Never underestimate politics in this area or, rather, the power of the

130

purse. If the Rugby Union is intransigent, financial action can be taken through the Sports Council.

TIME FOR BATH TO FACE UP TO THEIR UNRULY FANS
The Observer, May 1987

I first noticed that the Bath supporters were different two years ago, when they came up to Twickenham to see their club deservedly (though unexcitingly) beat London Welsh in the cup. It may have been the contrast between the followers of the two clubs which made this difference so apparent.

The Welsh were predominantly middle-aged, of a certain gravity of demeanour, many with their wives and offspring. Mr Jones (Chemistry) said a polite good-afternoon to Mr Davies (Gym), while Mr Kinnock (Politics) was there with Mrs Kinnock (Infants) and the family to place a final seal of respectability upon the occasion. The Bath supporters, on the other hand, were much younger, some little more than children. They jostled and scuffled – admittedly with one another. But it was not very nice if you were old and frail and one of them crashed backwards into you. It was not specially agreeable if you were a middle-aged man of over 13 stone such as myself. At shops and off-licences on the way to the ground they disregarded queues, crowding with much effing and blinding around the counter. From time to time a dozen or so would break into a trot, not specially menacing, but again not very pleasant if you were old and they were running towards you.

A year ago, when Bath played Wasps in the final, I noticed that these characteristics had become intensified – maybe on account of the continuing success of the club. In addition more senior supporters, people who, in the teacher's phrase, 'were old enough to know better', were displaying much noisiness and aggression.

Eight days ago, when their club defeated Wasps in the cup for the second year running, the younger element invaded the pitch when there were two minutes to go. The referee, Fred Howard, took the players off on the advice or instructions – it was not clear precisely which – of Dudley Wood, the Rugby Union's secretary.

Most people who were not at the match fail to realise that there were two separate invasions. The first occurred after Bath's final try and before Stuart Barnes had taken the conversion. Indeed, the ball had been purloined and had to be retrieved (or another one substituted) before he could make his attempt. The second invasion occurred immediately Barnes put the kick over. It is worth clarifying this because a single massed charge after a successful conversion would have been at least explicable, though not justifiable. After all, the digital clock on the advertising panel – a monument to the new-found commercial vulgarity and greed of the Rugby Union – was showing 47 minutes. The Bath children might have thought the match was at an end. But invading the pitch before the conversion demonstrated an ignorance of the laws of the game, to say nothing of the law of the land.

I took no pleasure in this spectacle. But I felt vindicated. Several months ago I wrote in *The Independent* that Bath's supporters were badly behaved. There was a lot of correspondence, which fell broadly into four categories. There were those who said that everyone had it in for Bath, players and supporters alike: this feeling of resentment was brought about by envy of the club's success. There were those who claimed that Bath's supporters were a fine body of young men, and more power – literally – to their elbows. There were those who maintained that, as a Welshman, I had no right to point to the bad behaviour of English supporters. And there were those who agreed with me. But several big-wigs in the Bath club cancelled their subscriptions.

Now, there is nothing to be gained by this surly, truculent refusal to face the obvious. Bad behaviour is not a problem for Bath alone but for much of the West Country. Gloucester supporters can be equally unpleasant. The followers of Somerset CCC's Sunday team act as if they have just been released from what used to be called a reformatory. One trouble is that the area, Bristol apart, does not boast any League soccer clubs to filter off the yobbish tendency. In the meantime, fathers might start accompanying their sons (and daughters also) to matches. And the Bath club, after last Saturday's evidence, might stop pretending that nothing was amiss.

PANIC IS NOT THE WAY TO MANAGE
The Independent, September 1987

Never underestimate an Englishman, my father used to advise me. He might look slow, but he was persistent, had application; he got there in the end. The Welsh, by contrast, embarked on enterprises of one kind or another with tremendous enthusiasm. Then they met with a few reverses and, easily discouraged, would retire from the field. They would return to their firesides to sulk, maintaining that they could easily have beaten the opposition – for they were, after all, clearly the better side – but that they did not think it was worth it. They would then ask Mam to pour another cup of tea, saying that they fancied egg and chips for dinner.

Though a patriotic Welshman, my father was a creator of national stereotypes who would have been instantly banned by the Lewisham Council. At the time he was dispensing his advice to me, however, 40-odd years ago, there was a good deal of truth in his generalisations, whether applied to rugby or to other, even more important fields of endeavour.

But in their response to the World Cup, the English have certainly not conformed to the model. The appointment of Mike Weston as a sort of manager strikes me as an act of panic, not an application of that cool, calm deliberation which, as Harold Macmillan used to like to remind his colleagues, unravels every knot. I write that Weston is a 'sort of' manager because he is not going to be given the powers which Sir Alf Ramsey, for example, used to possess. It is all very odd. England's performances last season and in the World Cup were (leaving the players out of account for the moment) primarily the responsibility of Weston and of the coach Martin Green. Time and again they were told where they were going wrong, both in this column and by more exalted authorities.

It was wrong to appoint Richard Hill virtually captain-for-life, rather as the Duke of Marlborough was made commander-for-life, and then to be stuck with someone who was manifestly not up to the job, whether as captain or as scrum-half.

It was a mistake to hail the thuggery of the French match as a sterling English performance, and not to anticipate the troubles of the Welsh match. It was a further error to attempt a half-hearted justification of the English team's behaviour on that muddied occasion.

And it was a humiliation to have the temporary dismissal of several English players forced on you by higher authority. I am usually chary of saying that people should resign. But I should have thought that a public reprimand by the Rugby Football Union to the coach and the chairman of selectors would have entailed the automatic resignation of both of them.

Then came the Scottish match, a false dawn and the World Cup. After last season and its sequel, there were three rational choices: to persist with the old system under the old names; to persist with the old system under new or juggled names, Weston, Green or both dropping out; or to embark on a new, managerial system under a new name. If the last choice had been adopted, the obvious candidate would have been Alan Davies of Nottingham, though Chalkie White, formerly of Leicester, and Jack Rowell of Bath would have had their supporters.

But there is nothing whatever to be said for starting a new era under an old and (to be frank) discredited name. Weston even tried to bring Green back into the magic circle, but was, it appears, frustrated in this attempt. I have no animus against Weston. As a centre and utility back he was a pundits' favourite. I thought him a rather boring player whose chief accomplishment was his ability to kick the ball higher than anyone else. When I now observe him at matches his handsome countenance usually bears a puzzled expression – as well it may.

The English are at least doing something, even if it is the wrong thing. The Welsh, on the other hand, are somewhat easily pleased. This is just as much a national characteristic as the disposition to be easily discouraged. But more of this in another column.

AN ECHO OF HQ's EMPTY GRANDEUR
The Independent, October 1987

Tomorrow Swansea come to Twickenham to play the Harlequins. It is a match that I rarely miss. It is usually bad-tempered but entertaining. The players have overcome the slack ways and buttery fingers which they display at the very beginning of any season. Mid-autumn being the best part of the year in Britain, the weather is often sunny.

One of my colleagues in Another Newspaper was, I noticed, suggesting the other day that Quins should play these early-season fixtures at their nearby ground, the Stoop Memorial (where they perforce play later in the season, when the international and representative matches are under way). I should regret this change, if it were ever made. Stoop is not my idea of a first class ground. With its small, solitary stand, it is more like Ammanford's accommodation. Proper first class grounds – Stradey Park, Llanelli, The Gnoll at Neath – are like Third Division football grounds.

Then again, I am fond of Twickenham, stands echoing, lavatories shut, restaurants still, bars shuttered. It is like a seaside resort after season, enabling the imagination to work. It is, I suppose, a matter of personal temperament. My guess is that Twickenham will be used for club matches at the beginning of a season for many years to come. It will see me out, I am fairly sure.

Will they, however, be the same matches: Llanelli (a sad disappointment two weeks ago) in mid-September, then Swansea, followed by Cardiff? The new league system is certainly going to bring about some rigidity. It may be – what would have been unthinkable a season ago – that to a native-born English supporter, as distinct from a Welsh expatriate, a league match between two English sides will prove more attractive than an Anglo-Welsh match signifying little or nothing. Last week, when Leicester played the Quins, the atmosphere at Twickenham was quite different from what it had been on the previous Saturday for the Llanelli match.

Llanelli supporters are knowledgeable and, on the whole, well behaved, though they have a tendency to lash out in a nasty way (verbally, I hasten to add, rather than physically) when things are not going too well for their boys, as they were certainly not going two weeks ago. But they do not travel. I do not mean that they do not travel well, but that they do not travel much.

For Leicester's supporters, on the other hand, the route to Twickenham is a well-worn road, owing to the club's numerous cup appearances over the past few years. Indeed, the game a week ago had all the atmosphere of a cup tie. The stands might still have been echoing, but they were echoing to a sound of genuine enthusiasm which has rarely, in the past, been heard so early in the season.

It would be a pity if the Anglo-Welsh fixtures turned into the equivalent of the current Anglo-Irish or -Scottish fixtures: virtually exhibition matches, played once in a while. But the logic of the league will, in the end, mean that the matches do go this way, unless some purposive action is taken.

England have a cup and now a league. Wales have a cup and are talking about a league. What about an additional Anglo-Welsh Cup? There could be 16 Welsh and 16 English clubs, the latter selected from the previous season's league placings. The competition would take up five Saturdays, though the first and second rounds could be played mid-week. The only rule would be that, at each stage, an English would meet a Welsh club. There would be no cheating, or 'seeding' as it is more politely termed. If Cardiff were drawn against Bath in the first round, that would be that. The final would be played at Twickenham or at the National Ground, Cardiff, alternating by the year. I tell you: if I were in commercial sponsorship, I should be a wealthy man.

THE STUFF OF WELSH ROMANCE
The Independent, October 1987

One of the stories I was brought up on concerned the young Wilfred Wooller when he was at Rydal School between the wars. One day, he got up in class and made for the door.

'What do you think you are doing, Wooller?' the master asked.

'Off to London, sir.'

'What are you going to do in London, Wooller?'

'Play for Wales, sir.'

The story cannot possibly be true in its details, though something like it may well have happened, for Wooller did win his first cap when he was very young. But it is a nice little story all the same, which it would be a pity to spoil. The old *Boys Own Paper* used to run similar tales regularly (for the BOP published quite a lot of rugby stories, unlike *Wizard* and *Hotspur*, which gave precedence to aviators, explorers and soccer players).

And Wales's experiences in the World Cup had some of the same qualities of schoolboy romance. It was not just that they came third, when most of us expected them to be beaten, not only by New Zealand, Australia and France but also by Scotland certainly and England possibly. It was also the manner of their success, with young men who happened to be in Australia, visiting their aunties or whatever, being picked off the streets, kitted out, and told that they would be playing for Wales tomorrow.

This was almost exactly what happened with Richard

Webster and David Young, both of Swansea. The front row of Young, Alan Phillips and Anthony Buchanan was not so much the second-choice trio as the third choice. Wales ended up with only three first-choice forwards available. Indeed, it would have paid any ambitious young Welsh player to mount a charity concert in his village hall to send him to Australia on the off-chance. All this was the stuff of schoolboy romance.

What was not romantic at all, what was rather horrible in fact, was the practice of carting players home, on the very next aeroplane, as soon as they did themselves an injury – irrespective, it seemed, of whether the injury was likely to right itself given time. I suppose the players can count themselves lucky that they were simply not taken round the corner and shot as if they were racehorses which had broken a leg. However, the Welsh authorities were by no means the most callous offenders in this respect.

Their offence is different. It is complacency; being too easily satisfied. There are understandable reasons for that state of mind. Wales came back top – in theory – of the home countries and in front of the admittedly disappointing Australia also. To be fair to the Welsh big-wigs (as I invariably endeavour to be), they did return with three world class players, footballers who would be in serious contention for a place in one of those World XVs so useful to bored schoolboys and desperate rugby writers. These were John Devereux, Jonathan Davies and, above all, Robert Jones. The other three home countries produced only one altogether, the Scot Gavin Hastings.

Since then, Devereux has injured himself walking through a plate-glass door while on holiday abroad, which does not seem a very clever thing to do, though it could, I suppose, happen to any of us. Davies has injured himself playing a Sunday sevens match – a frivolous activity at the best of times, in my opinion, but certainly not one in which the Welsh outside-half ought to involve himself at the beginning of a season. While Jones is in and out of the Swansea side under their rota policy. Last Saturday, he was a replacement against Harlequins and went on as a centre. These citizens will all, presumably, be fit for the internationals.

138

But Wales have numerous problems, particularly in the pack. What Ian Eidman's crime was I have yet to discover, passed over as he was in favour, first, of Stuart Evans and then of Steve Blackmore and, most recently, Young. At the same time the selectors persist at No 8 with Phil Davies, who is no more than an average club player. Still, it was romantic to come third in the World Cup. This is where I suspect they will end up in the Five Nations championship as well.

WRITERS LOST FOR WORDS IN BOOKS
The Independent, October 1987

For a change, this week I thought we might try to get away from the subjects that tend to dominate rugby discussion at this time of year, before the start of the international championship. These subjects include (in no particular order): South Africa, shamateurism, team managers, dirty play and whether the English county sides any longer serve a purpose. One old faithful has gone. Or, rather, it has lost its speculative appeal, because it is now with us. I mean, of course, the league; or the semi-league, which is all it is ever likely to be.

Instead I should like to turn from the players and administrators to those who write about the game, whether full-time or, as I do, part-time. My question is: why should writing about rugby turn out so very differently from writing about cricket?

I ask in a spirit less of criticism than of curiosity. I certainly intend no adverse criticism of my colleagues in the Press box, who can tell me without hesitation that it was the No 4 who scored the push-over try – who can do it, moreover, without benefit of field glasses and before the scorer's name has come over the loudspeaker. The standard of daily and weekly reporting, and of comment also, is as high as it is in cricket.

Yet there is no literature of rugby, as there is a literature of cricket. There are many books, and quite a few good ones. A pioneer in the social analysis of the game was *Report on Rugby*, by Geoffrey Nicholson and John Morgan, which was published in 1959, but, as far as I remember, created little stir at the time. The Welsh Rugby Union adopted a similar approach, hiring two academic historians to write their centenary history. The 1970s, following the golden – or perhaps it was the silver – age of British rugby, saw the publication of numerous good autobiographies of players. As in the case of Peter Wright and *Spycatcher*, however, we heard little about the merits of the work in question and much about the penalties to be visited upon its author. It is a national characteristic that we are less interested in what someone said than in whether he had any business to say it. Then there are the diaries, whether of home seasons or of overseas tours. I recently enjoyed two from this category, one by Frank Keating, the other by Gerald Davies and John Morgan. David Parry-Jones has, in *Taff's Acre*, edited a successful symposium by old Cardiff players on the Arms Park over the years. Alun Richards has written a moving memoir of Carwyn James. These are just a few of the books I have read with pleasure over the past few years.

But rugby, though it may grip the imagination, does not grip the literary imagination – or not to the same degree as cricket. Great rugby players are rarely the subjects of full biographies as great cricketers are. There are umpteen anthologies of notable writings on cricket, but hardly any of writings on rugby. Cricket set-pieces, from Dickens to MacDonnell, are served up time and again. There are no comparable rugby set-pieces. As a schoolboy at Dulwich, P. G. Wodehouse was as good at rugby as he was at cricket. To the end of his days he followed the fortunes of the college XV. But the 'Mike' books are about cricket. In his later works, he wrote a little about boxing, much about golf, nothing about rugby.

If we turn from the world of the imagination to that of fact, it is the same story (though I would make an exception for John Griffiths's *Book of English International Rugby*). Followers of cricket are better served. *Rothmans Rugby Yearbook* is invaluable, and God bless all who sail in her. But she is not

Wisden. Indeed, it tells us something that this is only the 16th year of publication. Statistics can be both tedious and misleading, I realise. Cricket is more susceptible of analysis than rugby. But I should like to know, for instance, not only the points totals for kickers, but their percentage totals, taking unsuccessful kicks into account. We may not be able to produce great literature. We should certainly be able to serve up more simple facts, particularly with all the new technology lying around.

UPS AND DOWNS OF A CLIMBER
The Independent, October 1987

This week I propose to write the brief life of a rugby player, R. H. Lloyd-Davies. He came from my native village, Tycroes, Carmarthenshire, and was seven years older than I was. His full name was Rheinallt Lloyd Hughes Davies, but he was known locally as Hugh Lloyd Davies. The initials and the hyphen came later, for Hugh, despite his many outstanding qualities, was a bit of a climber. His family owned one of the two bus companies operating from the village, Tycroes being particularly well-endowed with this form of enterprise. Though the family were prosperous, they were not ostentatious or grand. His father worked as a conductor on the family buses to give himself an occupation.

Hugh, along with his brother and sister, attended the Amman Valley County (subsequently Grammar) School, Ammanford. When he went up to Cambridge later, and was asked where he had been at school, he would reply: 'Amma*n*ford, actually', placing the accent on the second syllable. A peculiarity of his childhood was that he was brought up by his grandparents, who lived just down the road, while his siblings remained with his parents. Anyway, it was said that Hugh was 'spoiled'. He was, however, denied a bicycle. He was told that, as he could travel free on the buses at any time he liked, he did not need a bicycle.

As a sixth-former he had an affair with the French mistress. This was prosecuted vigorously during bouts of fire-watching, a duty which teachers and senior pupils were required to undertake. They married when he was in his early twenties. Hugh had always enjoyed (or suffered from) a sexual drive well above the average. Like most successful practitioners in this field, he was both bold and undiscriminating. He was also handsome, with pale, smooth skin, black curly hair that grew in a peak, very bright eyes and very white teeth. He possessed loads of charm. In drink, however, he could turn verbally vicious.

He was a fast, adventurous full-back, and a schoolboy international. From school he was conscripted into the RAF, where he soon became a pilot officer. He played in the great inter-service and representative matches at St Helen's, Swansea, and for Wales, first against New Zealand, the 1945 Kiwis, and then against England in the 1946 Victory International. In neither match were his experiences particularly happy. Against New Zealand he kicked the ball straight at J. R. Sherratt, who promptly scored. Against England another wing, R. H. Guest, evaded him to score two tries. Hugh resented the non-award of caps for this match, and kept claiming — what was morally true but factually incorrect — that he was a Welsh international. However, he confidently expected to be in the post-war side. But the selectors preferred Frank Trott of Cardiff, less spectacular but much safer.

From the RAF, Hugh went up to Trinity Hall, Cambridge, to read law. He won the university match of 1947 by kicking two penalties, six points to Oxford's nil. On the morning of the game he had been roused from a deep slumber by two friends, given a shower, dressed and poured on to the team coach. Shortly afterwards he was sent down from the university. He was in a pub, a proctor arrived, and ordered him to leave. The proctor, Trevor Thomas, was not only a law don at Hugh's college but came from Swansea. Hugh addressed him familiarly in Welsh, telling him not to be so silly. Thomas was not amused.

Nevertheless he joined Gray's Inn and played for London

Welsh and Harlequins, where, he said, you met a better class of girl. Finding himself short of money, he joined Barrow – the first Cambridge Blue to go north. He was paid £1,000, played a couple of matches and then promptly decamped to Paris.

Returning to London, he had several encounters with the law, culminating in a nine months' prison sentence for attempting to pawn stolen jewellery. During the early 1950s, he was in Tycroes, doing odd labouring jobs. He then went back to London. There were reports of sightings. He was passing himself off as a colonel; had gone bald; was sleeping rough; was a gardener with the Islington council. A few months ago, I was told that he had died last year.

A MODEL MODERN MANAGER
The Independent, October 1987

For well over a decade we have lived in the age of the coach. We may now be entering the age of the manager. Suddenly they are popping up all over the place like mushrooms – and some, such as the unfortunate Mike Weston, are being plucked early and eaten for breakfast. We all know the disadvantages of managers as a class. Football managers I have always thought of (with a few exceptions) as risible figures, with their alternation between heroic and villainous status, their gold jewellery, and their imperfect grasp of grammar and syntax. This may be snobbish of me but there it is: it cannot be helped.

There is, however, a more serious case against managers. In a sense, the more forceful they are, the stronger is that case. It is that they crush individuality and take the fun out of life. This case could be, and indeed was, made against rugby coaches. And yet, coaching has been on the whole a success. It has been at its most successful when great coaches, such as the late Carwyn James, were enabled to work with good players, such as the 1971 Lions or the Llanelli side of the same period.

143

Individuals matter more than systems: a truism, but true. Whether James would have made a manager I rather doubt. He was so disorganised in his life that he would certainly have needed the assistance of a deputy to look up the timetables.

Brian Thomas of Neath is, I would guess, a very different character from James: a Cambridge metallurgist, not an Aberystwyth Welsh scholar; a forward, not a back; a realist, not a romantic. On the evidence of this and last season, however, Thomas, as manager, has done as much for Neath as James, as coach, did for Llanelli and the British Isles 16 years ago. Indeed, it is arguable that, because he had less promising material to work on initially, his achievement is the more remarkable. The departure of two outstanding players, Jonathan Davies and Stuart Evans, has made no difference.

Thomas himself was an uncompromising lock – that is the word which is trotted out on these occasions, uncompromising. He was unlucky not to go with the 1966 Lions to New Zealand. And Neath have always had the reputation of being a robust side – another of those words, robust. Later, Rees Stephens introduced rucking to Neath following his (and the late Roy John's) return from the New Zealand tour of 1950. Having regard to this weight of the past, one would have expected Thomas to base his policy on forward domination. Not so.

The Neath forwards (who, along with the whole club, operate under a rota system) are not specially big. They look rather like a valley pack of the 1950s, which may be a consequence of the short-back-and-sides style of haircut favoured by the majority of them. But they are certainly faster, and fitter, than forwards were in those days. Their success comes from support, from speed to the breakdown and from making the ball available. They will ruck if they have to. But, unlike New Zealand sides, they do not ruck merely for the sake of it. They prefer to transfer the ball to the backs as quickly as possible, by hand if this is more convenient. Since the departure of Jonathan Davies, none of the halves or three-quarters is really outstanding. But they are prepared to have a go from anywhere, and score numerous tries in the process.

Neath's style is preferable to Wales's lack of style. Thomas should be given a chance to run the national side. Knowing the Welsh Rugby Union, I would add that pigs might fly.

NOT THE GOOD REF GUIDE
The Independent, November 1987

A few weeks ago I suggested to a colleague in the sports department of this paper that I might write a column, to be entitled provisionally 'The Good Ref Guide'. 'That will be a very short column,' he replied. Nevertheless, I have been following the controversy about British referees in the World Cup, particularly Clive Norling, with a certain detached interest. It is detached both because I was several thousand miles away at the time and because I tend to judge my countrymen with perhaps too much severity. To adapt Dr Johnson: 'The Welsh are a fair people; they never speak well of one another.'

Norling still seems to be the best referee not only in these islands but also, from the evidence of television, in the world. There was a marked decline in the standard when either of the Australian referees, Fordham and Fitzgerald, was in charge. I think Roger Quittenton of England was shabbily treated too. I do not share the prejudice of my fellow countrymen against Quittenton. His trouble is not that he is an incompetent referee but that he is too pleased with himself, or anyway appears to be so. While most of his colleagues resemble suet puddings, he gives the impression of being a West End actor who has seen better times, and is now spending the autumn of his days playing in rep in Richmond.

Norling is no suet pudding either. Indeed, I would describe him as a fine figure of a man. But the reason given for sending him home early was that he was 'too fat' to referee in the concluding stages. If referees are to be judged in this way, what about players? Gareth Chilcott of Bath would be permanently barred on aesthetic grounds. Incidentally, I

145

have a friend who takes his two small sons to matches. They are at the age when other people's physical characteristics are a subject for much mirth. When they become bored with the game, they scan the crowd for generously-proportioned ladies, saying ungallantly: 'Look, Dad, there's Chilcott's sister.'

However, there is something faintly depressing about boasting that we produce the best referees. It is rather like claiming, as it is often claimed, that we are the leading nation for company liquidators and trustees in bankruptcy. We should certainly not be complacent. From my observation this season, our referees have several failings. They are over-strict about some things and overindulgent about others.

Forward passes are now allowed regularly, particularly where there is a traditional, flowing movement ending with a try or with the player's being forced into touch near the line. It is as if the referee is reluctant to spoil the fun. This is an excellent principle, as the best of all post-war referees, D. Gwynne Walters, fully realised. But it should be applied by an imaginative use of the advantage law and by a reluctance to niggle. A forward pass is not a niggle.

Again, throws into the lineout are now usually successful exercises in deceiving the referee. The deception is rendered easier by their habit of standing several yards to one side of the 90-degree line along which the hooker (usually) is meant to be throwing. The reason is supposed to be that, by so positioning himself, the referee avoids being in the way. A moment's thought will show that the chance of being in the way is unchanged, even increased, because the action takes place on one side or the other, rarely in the middle.

On the other hand, referees penalise dangerous tackles when they are not dangerous at all, but merely on the high side. Last Saturday, Julian Davies of London Welsh was penalised for a dangerous tackle when he was trying to charge down a kick. Much more serious, however, are the penalties for being over the top, killing the ball, failing to release. John Griffiths's recently-published *Phoenix Book of International Rugby Records* tells part of the story.

The record points-scorers, the Ollie Campbells and Dusty

Hares, are all kickers of recent years. Even comparative newcomers, such as Gavin Hastings, Paul Thorburn and Rob Andrew, are already statistical immortals owing to their feats with the boot. The great try-scorers, by contrast, are from the past. But for a change, we will have to alter the laws, not the scoring system.

THE FLY HALF ON THE WALL
The Independent, November 1987

This column was lucky enough to overhear an informal conversation among three of the Welsh selectors, Rod Morgan, the chairman (South Wales Police), Derek Quinnell (Llanelli) and David Richards (Swansea), following Wales's win over the American Eagles.

'I think,' Quinnell said, 'I am beginning to get the hang of your policy, Rod, although it has taken a long time to sink in.'

'Thank you, Derek. I seem to remember you had a similar difficulty with Carwyn James when you were playing on the blind side for the Lions in 1971.'

'What I was told,' Richards interjected, 'was that Carwyn said you had to stop Sid Going, and you said: "Which one is Going?", and Carwyn replied: "He is the one with No 9 on his back. Just remember No 9, Derek, and you will not go far wrong".'

'That is broadly correct, David, although I would not wish to confirm the story in all its details.'

'Unfortunately, boys,' Morgan said, 'selection policy is not such a simple matter. What would you say we are up to, David?'

'Well, first of all, we are trying to discover talent wherever it can be found, particularly among policemen, while not forgetting the interests of great clubs such as Swansea and Llanelli.'

'What I think we are trying to do, Rod,' Quinnell added, 'is to confuse the opposition. That has always been an important aspect of the game, in my opinion.'

'I certainly prefer Derek's way of putting it to yours, David, although I do not wish to have a quarrel with you at this stage of the evening. At centre, for example, we were placed in a difficult position, because John Devereux had injured himself walking through a plate-glass door when he was on his holidays.'

'That is the sort of behaviour I would have expected of an English centre, Rod. A Welsh centre should have learnt to avoid obstacles of that nature at an early stage of his career.'

'It is all very well to talk, Dai, but you were a great one for avoiding obstacles throughout your playing life, as I remember. You never made a tackle if you could get out of it, or were tackled yourself if you could help it.'

Quinnell attempted the part of peacemaker.

'Now, boys, there is no need to talk like that. I am still waiting for Rod to explain his plan to us.'

'Certainly, Derek. Mark Ring has been playing as outside-half for Pontypool, so naturally we pick him as a centre. Bleddyn Bowen has been a centre for his country, so naturally we pick him at outside-half.'

'And when Tony Clement comes on as a substitute, who is normally an outside-half, he plays as a centre.'

'That is right, David. I think you have got the point, which is that, as Derek says, we are trying to confuse the opposition by playing our boys in unexpected positions.'

'Stuart Russell of London Welsh is a case in point.'

'That was a brilliant move, Derek. Russell is normally a No 8 for his club, although he has played as a No 6 flanker. So we confuse everybody by turning him into a lock.'

'In the next game we can put him in the front row.'

'If that was a joke, Derek, it was not funny. I know it was tried with your colleague Delme Thomas, and also with Ian Jones, but neither experiment was a success.'

'You seem to forget, Rod, that I won about half the caps I should have done because I was always being shifted around between No 6, No 8 and lock, and I do not wish the same fate to befall another young man, such as Russell. Or Paul Moriarty either, for that matter.'

'It was the same with me, although not so bad,' Richards

added. 'When I was an outside-half they said I was really a centre, and when I was a centre that I was really an outside-half.'

'But Brian Thomas of Neath is forever shifting his players about, in the forwards anyway. In the last few matches alone, Kevin Phillips, the hooker, has played as a flanker and as a prop. When Thomas does this, he is praised to the skies in the newspapers as an exponent of total rugby, whatever that may be exactly, whereas when we do it, we are attacked for muddle and confusion.'

'There is no justice in the world, Rod,' Quinnell said.

A PAST MASTER STAND-OFF
The Independent, November 1987

What we call a buzz, the Victorians call a hum. Hums were started quite cynically by 19th-century politicians. 'Shall we have a hum about Mr Gladstone's retirement?' they would ask. In the English rugby world today, there is a hum about the recall of Les Cusworth. There is nothing at all cynical in this, I hasten to add. It is wholly sincere. Cusworth almost certainly is the best outside-half now playing in England.

He rarely makes the wrong choice. He is a good punter, an even better drop-kicker. He does a valiant job behind a pack who are not perhaps the force they were; certainly they are not when Dean Richards is absent (though John Wells remains an underestimated flanker). Yes, I would pick Cusworth. And, yes, I agree with Peter Wheeler when he says that you cannot forever be building for a future which never comes and that the selectors' job is to win the next match. And yet ... and yet ... if Cusworth is selected along with Richard Harding, England will be starting the championship with halves born respectively in 1953 and 1954. Even John Rutherford was born in 1955.

If Cusworth is chosen, there is a sense in which the selectors, whoever they may turn out to be – so far only two have emerged from the undergrowth – will be atoning for the sins of their predecessors. For, there is no doubt about it, Cusworth has been appallingly treated. His international career to date has spanned 1979-84. He has played only one full international season, 1984.

In England, there are usually three or four players around who are more or less up to the job, and the selectors cannot make up their minds whom to choose. In Wales, by contrast, a period of competition between two players or, alternatively, of cosmic confusion is succeeded by the emergence of one usually great outside-half.

Thus the uncertainty about whether to choose Billy Cleaver or Glyn Davies was succeeded by the domination of Cliff Morgan. The reign of Morgan was followed by baronial wars, until the succession descended on David Watkins. Watkins, after a brief struggle, gave way to the mightiest sovereign of all, Barry John. He abdicated, however, when he was only 26, in favour of Phil Bennett, who, after a successful reign – with the brief interregnum of the late John Bevan – transferred the crown to Gareth Davies.

Unhappily the reign of Davies was marred towards its close by the preference for Malcolm Dacey evinced by Bevan (by now a power behind the throne). Davies abdicated in disgust. But the throne left empty by him was not filled by the usurper Dacey. Another Davies, Jonathan, had appeared in the kingdom. 'Lo, we have another King,' the simple folk of Wales cried in exultation and relief. The signs are, however, that after two years of virtually uninterrupted reign by Jonathan, the wise men behind the throne – Rod Morgan and friends – are beginning to have doubts. They are going into one of those periods of gloomy introspection to which the Welsh are prone.

Davies was overpraised too early (true, as I pointed out at the time, but that was hardly the poor boy's fault). He said imprudent things about going north and making a lot of money to buy himself a nice house. He fell out with Neath. His freedom from injury is in doubt. He has not played much this season. And so on. Bleddyn Bowen, Mark Ring and even the young Anthony Clement are all being canvassed as replacements. Yet Davies still arouses genuine apprehension in opponents – besides being a draw on his own. If England would be imprudent to omit Cusworth, Wales would be very silly indeed not to choose Davies.

OTI CUTS A PROLIFIC FIGURE

The Independent, December 1987

I had never before seen a crowd at Twickenham rise spontaneously to a player as the West Stand rose to Chris Oti when he went off injured in the university match. He certainly earned his reception. I did not think he would score his first try, because the Oxford cover were out in force. Indeed, from where I was sitting at the other end of the field, it seemed to me that the defenders outnumbered the Cambridge attackers.

There are some sour persons who say he did not 'really' score at all, because he hit the cornerflag first. There are others (though usually they are the same persons) who claim he did not 'really' score his second try either, because there had been a forward pass. One of these grudging souls, did, however, manage a joke, to the effect that Roger Quittenton was clearly trying to be invited to umpire in Pakistan. He was not, as it happened, a Welshman (Quittenton's chief persecutors by custom and practice) but a Merseyside Conservative MP who had been at Oxford.

But by any standards they were two remarkable scores. It is worth remembering also that Oti scored the solitary try in last year's equivalent match, when the cry 'Give the ball to Oti' could be heard in the stands. For more than a year it has been manifest that, in him, England have an already outstanding and possibly great wing. If another black player, Martin Offiah, had stayed instead of going to Rugby League (where he is the leading try-scorer), England would have have had a luxury of choice in this position.

Is it conceivable that Rory Underwood, who has the

reputation of being world class, and is still only 24, should now be dropped in Oti's favour? I think it is. In fact, I would go further, and argue that – quite apart from Oti's appearance on the scene – Underwood's record so far does not justify his seemingly automatic selection on England's left wing. This is not to question his speed, his power or the excitement which he generates in the crowd. What it is to question is his ability to score tries when it matters and when he has the chance to do so.

But which wings, you may ask, are now given the chance? An answer is that Mike Harrison, for one, both makes and takes half chances. With the aid of John Griffiths's invaluable *Phoenix Book of International Rugby Records*, the figures are fairly easy to work out.

Let us divide the number of tries scored by the number of matches played by the wing in question. We may call the ratio so obtained the strike-rate. C. N. Lowe comes top with 18 tries in 25 matches, a strike-rate of 0.72. The second most productive wing of recent times is Harrison himself, with equivalent figures of 7, 12, 0.58. Number three may surprise you. He is Simon Smith, who was unjustly dropped (along with Jamie Salmon and Simon Halliday) after the Scottish match in 1986 and has hardly appeared even for Wasps so far this season. His figures are 4, 9, 0.44.

Underwood, by contrast, has played 17 times for England and scored four tries, of which two were against Japan in the World Cup (though, to be fair, Harrison's three in that match bumped up his average also). Underwood's strike-rate is 0.24. Of established England wings, only Peter Squires has a worse record with three tries, 29 matches, 0.10 strike-rate.

Some wings have no strike-rate at all, because they never managed to score. They include David Trick, Tony Swift and Mark Bailey – who did, however, score one try against Japan when no caps were being awarded. After Smith in strike-rate is Ted Woodward, 0.40; then Dickie Guest 0.38; followed by Peter Jackson, 0.30; Peter Thompson, 0.29; David Duckham 0.28; John Carleton, 0.27; and Mike Slemen, 0.26.

The only surprise among these figures is the high position occupied by Simon Smith. In justice, he should have been preferred to both Underwood and his club-mate Bailey over the past few years. Not that figures mean everything or, indeed, anything very much. But they are interesting nevertheless and, on the evidence of the university match, I would expect Chris Oti to beat everybody except Cyril Lowe, who, after all, belonged to a different era.

PASSING OUT THE PRESENTS
The Independent, December 1987

This is the time of year for distributing presents. The lucky recipients are not, by and large, the rich, the powerful and the successful, who do not need them. Rather, they are the unfortunate and the unsuccessful, or those who, for one reason or another, would benefit from a particular gift.

Prominent among the latter group is Rod Morgan, the chairman of the Welsh selectors. He receives a leatherbound copy of *Illusion and Reality*, for saying (or at least allowing it to be said on his behalf) that Wales are now the third best Rugby Union side in the world.

His colleagues receive copies, not leatherbound, of *The Amateur Juggler: Fun for all the Family*. This follows their selection of Stuart Russell, normally a No 8, as a lock; of Mark Ring, now an outside-half, as a centre; and of various other players chosen to perform in unfamiliar positions.

Llanelli have always made a speciality of spoiling players' careers by messing them about. It happened to Peter Morgan. More recently, it happened to that potentially very good player Kevin Thomas, of whom little has been seen this season. And it may now be happening to Ieuan Evans, who has been almost equally obscure from view owing to injury. There is no present for Llanelli this Christmas, I am afraid. But Cardiff receives a new outside-half, and Newport a nomination for the year's Nobel Peace Prize.

Across the border, Mike Weston gets the traditional gold watch both in recognition of past services and as an indication that they will not be required in the future. If he wanted to retain the help of Tony Jorden and Martin Green, he should have made it clear before accepting the new post of manager. Alternatively, the English rugby authorities should have made it clear to him that he would not be in a position to reappoint his chums before they confirmed him in the job. This bears out one of my maxims: if there is a way in which a sporting authority can cause chaos, cause it they will. There are no exceptions (see the cases of the Football League and Mr Maxwell, and the TCCB and Mr Gatting).

Weston's successor, Geoff Cooke, receives a copy of that rare and scarce work, *Rugby Can Be Fun Too*. It is widely suspected that Green seized and destroyed the few copies which remained at headquarters.

My next present is an apology to J. V. Smith, until recently president of the Rugby Union. Inexplicably, I omitted him from my discussion of England wings last week. He gained four caps in 1949-50 and scored four tries. This gives him a strike-rate of 1.0, which is, I think, the highest of the lot.

The last present goes to Nigel Starmer-Smith. It is a selection of plain, rather subdued ties, to replace his present somewhat distracting striped collection. He gets his present for trying and for putting up with a lot of adverse criticism. I am glad to see Chris Rea on the programme, but sorry to miss Ian Robertson. It is now acquiring a surrealist aspect. Last Sunday there was an attractive young lady embracing a goalpost and pretending to be a hooker, of the front row variety, I mean. Young ladies are fine, and women's rugby is doubtless to be encouraged. But would not a more gnarled specimen – Mr Wheeler, say – be more instructive to the young, even though less attractive?

TACKLING RUGBY'S PHONEYS
The Independent, January 1988

For the last few days, the rugby news and comment in the papers has, quite properly, been about the international selectors and their choices for the coming championship. As a change, I should like to discuss people who claim that they were members of various more or less distinguished teams in the past – in other words, rugby bullshitters. For some reason, this form of boasting, romancing or fantasising is more common among rugby followers than it is among those of other sports. Notice that I do not use the word 'lying'.

Your true rugby bullshitter is not, usually, a liar in his daily existence. He is often a model citizen. The chap who claims he had a trial for Swansea in 1957 is commonly a person who would tell an untruth, if he told one at all, only to the Inland Revenue.

Incidentally, the claim of having had a trial, as distinct from having actually played in the team, is a sure sign of the authentic bullshitter. First, such claims are difficult to check. Second, they indicate a becoming modesty – 'didn't make it to the first team, I'm afraid' – which, so the bullshitter vainly imagines, lends a verisimilitude to his claim.

Not that confirmation is always easy even when claims to membership of the first team are made. First class rugby provides no record of players comparable to *Wisden* in cricket. This is one reason for the relative popularity of rugby bullshitting. Another reason is that the activity is tolerated, even accepted up to a point. As John Young, the former Harlequins and England wing, and English selector, once put it to me: 'When someone says that he was with Waterloo before the war, we don't ask too many questions.'

A political, or lobby, correspondent I knew claimed to have played centre for the Quins. Despite his excessive weight and thick spectacles, he had, so I was told by common acquaintances, been a good hockey and cricket player in his youth. So his claim was not entirely impossible, though it still struck me as implausible. Moreover, I had regularly watched the Quins during the years, the mid-1960s, in which he would have turned out for them. I could not remember either his name on the programme or his form on the field.

In fact, I remembered who the centres were for the period in question. They were Tim Rutter and Bob Lloyd. And my acquaintance from the House of Commons lobby was certainly neither of these. Though I was not obsessed by the matter, I mentioned it to a friend, a former Quins player, later a club selector. He had no recollection whatever of my chum. If he had played even for the third team, he said, he would have remembered him.

Then there was the case of the former Labour MP who was standing at a by-election in Wales a few years ago. His campaign literature stated that he was a keen rugby follower who had played for Llanelli. I could not remember him at all. My colleagues who were covering the contest, however, accepted his claim uncritically. By polling day, he was being depicted as a cross between Albert Jenkins and Barry John. Perhaps justly, he lost. But I never summoned up the courage to ask him straight out whether he had really played for Llanelli.

Even the *Dictionary of National Biography* is not exempt. In his contribution on the author, editor and MP Frank Owen, Michael Foot states that Owen won a Cambridge Blue. But this is not confirmed by the records of the time.

Perhaps the best comment was made by Dylan Thomas, in 'A Story':

'I played for Aberavon in 1898,' said a stranger to Enoch Davies.

'Liar,' said Enoch Davies.

'I can show you photos,' said the stranger.

'Forged,' said Enoch Davies.

'And I'll show you my cap at home.'

'Stolen.'

'I got friends to prove it,' the stranger said in a fury.

'Bribed,' said Enoch Davies.

DOCTOR'S DISEASE RUNS RIFE

The Independent, January 1988

My old history master used to say that one of the chief characteristics of our system of government was that we did not bump people off. 'We do not even want to bump Dr Jack Matthews off,' he would add, to emphasise his point. 'Bump him, maybe, but not bump him off.' For 'Dr Jack', as he was called with a mixture of affection and derision, was not originally regarded as the ferocious crash-tackler of rugby legend. That reputation came after the Lions tour of New Zealand in 1950. In the Carmarthenshire of the late 1940s he was the centre who dropped the ball.

Bleddyn Williams we were prepared to admire, even idolise, despite his being a Cardiff player, but Dr Jack, from the same club, was something of a comic character, with his squat frame, his snub nose, his heavily brilliantined hair combed straight back and his show-off habit of holding the ball by its tip, with one hand. His historic function was to mess up whatever smart moves Bleddyn had initiated. It may have been unfair, but this was the opinion that the *aficionados* of west Wales used to hold about Jack Matthews.

I was reminded of him by the performance of the English centres last Saturday. Neither has his pugnacious personality, but Will Carling is even faster than he was, while Kevin Simms is considerably more elusive. The quality all three share is an inability to score tries. Simms is not a big man by modern standards, but at slightly over 12 stone he is big enough, I should have thought, to force himself over the line when he has only a few yards to go, instead of giving a somewhat despairing pass. One has only to imagine what Gareth Edwards – a player of similar size, though of greater physical strength – would have made of a similar opportunity. Carling, likewise, had several chances (admittedly not so obvious), which he failed to take.

Do not misunderstand me. Carling and Simms are very good players. Geoff Cooke and chums can count themselves lucky that they are second choices, or rather, third and fourth choices. The problem which the selectors now have is whether to restore John Buckton and Simon Halliday, one or both, to the places they occupied before the final trial.

The other problem – though hardly any of my esteemed colleagues seem to number it as such – is whether to replace Jon Webb with Simon Hodgkinson or Marcus Rose. I have never entirely understood the antipathy to Rose which undoubtedly exists among both commentators and spectators. He is like the villain in the Victorian melodrama, the character the audience have come to hiss.

When asked for a rational justification for their hostility, his critics reply that he is 'too slow'. Yet he is quick enough to play occasionally as stand-off half for the Harlequins, in which position he is slightly more impressive than Richard Cramb, who must be the luckiest international since Tony O'Reilly was recalled to play against England in 1970 at an advanced age. 'Too slow' is now flung at full-backs as a kind of catch-all rugby equivalent of conduct prejudicial to good order and military discipline. It used to be said about Paul Thorburn without any real justification.

The point is, however, that Rose, like Thorburn, kicks goals and wins matches. If he had been in the England team in Paris last Saturday he would, I feel sure, have kicked at least one of those which Webb missed. Accordingly, England would have won 12-10. Conceivably he would have kicked them all, and England would have won 18-10. People often talk as if there is a conflict between open rugby and having someone like Rose, who can actually kick, in the side. There is, on the contrary, no conflict at all.

England lost on Saturday because they neither scored tries which Simms and Carling should have taken nor kicked goals which Webb should have put over. The players I feel sorry for are the English forwards – even though John Orwin got away with some staggering lineout infringements which the luckless referee also missed. I have not seen his leniency in this regard referred to by the English rugby correspondents.

ROBERTS LEFT IN THE COLD
The Independent, January 1988

It was a decade ago, I suppose, when I first saw a 19-year-old student called Gareth Roberts play flanker for Swansea. Even then, he possessed speed, determination and football intelligence. It would be only a matter of time, I assumed, before he supplanted the then open-side incumbent, Rhodri Lewis, in the Welsh side. In the 1980s Roberts would, it seemed evident, be given the assured position occupied in the preceding four decades by (in reverse order of time) John Taylor, Haydn Morgan, Clem Thomas and Bob Evans.

Well, it did not happen. Roberts was in and out of the Swansea back row, owing partly to the club's squad policy, but partly also to a distinct preference by someone in the club for Mark Davies. The Welsh selectors showed the same preference – for a short time. On the whole they settled on David Pickering of Llanelli, who was given a variety of partners, from his obscure club-mate Alun Davies through the now largely forgotten Martyn Morris to Richard Moriarty, who, even on the blind side, is as much a flanker as I am a prima ballerina.

After this disappointing start, Roberts moved to Cardiff. In olden times this was thought to be the sure way for a gifted west Wales player to secure a cap. Now the move seems, if anything, disadvantageous. Roberts, at any rate, did not prosper either with his country or with his new club. Cardiff tended to switch him between Nos 6 and 7 – as Wales have done on the infrequent occasions when they have chosen him.

His first cap came in March 1985, when he should have been a fixture in the side for at least two years, as a replacement against France. His first real cap came in the following match, against England. He partnered Pickering and scored a try in a Welsh win. It seems incredible, but he did not play again for Wales until the World Cup last year. He appeared in five of the six matches and scored two tries, against both England, and, most crucially, Australia. Another scorer in that match was Paul Thorburn, likewise dropped against England, who kicked two penalties and two conversions.

Most observers returning from Australasia listed the competition's Welsh successes as, first, Robert Jones, and then, in no particular order, Thorburn, Roberts and John Devereux. Moreover, Roberts has scored three tries in six full international appearances. This gives him a strike-rate of 0.5, which is higher than that of most wings. Flankers, I realise, are no longer expected to score tries but, rather, to be industrious. No one could accuse Roberts of lacking application.

Consider: it has been plain for years that Wales have failed to win anything in the Five Nations championship because they lacked a good pack and, in particular, a good back row. Along comes the World Cup in which they finish a perhaps fortunate third but which does produce a decent Welsh back row for the first time in years: Roberts, Paul Moriarty and Richie Collins. The selectors promptly dropped Roberts, giving as their reason, privately, that his supplanter, Rowland Phillips of Neath, 'stays on his feet'.

The truth is, I fear, that Rod Morgan and friends see April 1989 ringed in heavy black on the calendar. If Wales do not win the championship either this year or next the 1980s will be the first decade since the 1880s in which they have not won it at least once. The result is that they have shown panic, bringing in the young, wholly inexperienced Anthony Clement at full-back even though Thorburn did all that was required of him, and more, in the World Cup – and dropping Roberts. The English stay loyal even to their failures; the Welsh are disloyal even to their successes.

A GAME OF ILL REPUTE
The Independent, February 1988

Last year's encounter between England and Wales was one of the most unpleasant games of rugby I have ever witnessed. It did considerable harm to the reputation of the sport in Britain. Not that its reputation was specially high last year in any case. Rugby in these islands reached its peak in the early 1970s and it has been downhill most of the way ever since. In the past nine months or so, however, a few snowdrops have been pushing through, even if a few snowdrops do not necessarily make a spring.

One was the World Cup – though the England-Wales

match proved one of the principal disappointments of the occasion. Another was the sprightly performance of England in their opening match in the Five Nations championship, and of Ireland likewise, come to that. And another was the new league system, which took most people by surprise with its initial success.

As we are on what is now termed the 'perceived image' of rugby, I should like to utter two grumbles, both connected with the World Cup. Once again, television not only let down rugby followers but also failed to realise that here was a sporting event which was watchable in its own right. My other grumble is that there was no official recognition of the success of the Welsh team. No one could accuse me of overindulgence towards my fellow countrymen, particularly those concerned with the administration of rugby football within the Principality. Certainly, some of the claims made afterwards for the Welsh side were fanciful.

This does not matter. Wales still came third. In these circumstances, it would have been pleasantly encouraging for the side to receive a message of congratulation from Mrs Margaret Thatcher. What was Denis up to? He is, after all, a former member of the London Society of Referees. Yet there was no word from No 10. Alternatively Peter Walker, the newly-appointed Welsh Secretary, could have sent a message or even held a reception, whether in London or in Cardiff. But when I mentioned the last possibility to him, he gave one of those polite but uneasy laughs which people tend to give when they think somebody has made a joke they do not quite understand. Walker clearly did not have any idea what I was talking about.

Neil Kinnock could now have stepped forward. In the past he has not been shy about proclaiming his enthusiasm for rugby. He could have done something, both as Leader of the Opposition and as a Welsh MP. When the Lions returned triumphantly from New Zealand in 1971, Jeffrey Thomas, then Member for Abertillery, held a reception in the Commons for the Welsh members of the party. On this more recent occasion neither Kinnock nor any other Welsh MP did anything, as far as I know. These receptions, I may say, I can take or leave. The majority of players, I suspect, share similar sentiments though perhaps different tastes. I nevertheless think that the official ignoring of the Welsh success in Australasia was insulting both to rugby football and to Wales.

These considerations will be far from the thoughts of the players who trot out at Twickenham tomorrow. Yet all the good work done by the World Cup can be undone not in minutes but in seconds. Of the miscreants dismissed from the England side after the match last year, only Wade Dooley is back in the 15 who will take the field. Of the Welsh forwards, those who keep their places are Norster, Moriarty and Collins (who went on after the injury to Phil Davies which caused most of the trouble).

The truth is, unhappily, that this has traditionally been a bad-tempered and sometimes vicious fixture. In 1947 I saw a Cardiff forward, a policeman, kick Micky Steele-Bodger. I am tempted to add: 'And who better, if you have to kick somebody?' But it was a nasty episode all the same. In 1980 the dismissal of Paul Ringer in the opening minutes soured the whole match.

Though I hope to see lots of running tomorrow, I expect realistically to see a match decided by penalties conceded by infringements in the lineout and the front row. I only trust the players keep both their fists and their feet approximately where they belong.

SUCCESS VEILS THE GAMBLE

The Independent, February 1988

In sport, as in politics and warfare, nothing succeeds like success. The winner takes all, from advertising contracts to television interviews. There is no reason for the observer of the passing scene to adopt the same grovelling attitude. It is in this independent spirit that I am happy for the Welsh team, in particular for Phil May (whose recognition, like Jeff Probyn's for England, has come about three years too late).

I congratulate Rod Morgan and friends, and now hope with somewhat greater realism they will win the Five Nations championship either this year or next. Otherwise Wales will, for the first time, have gone a decade without such a win. But I do not unsay anything of what I have written about Welsh selection policy. Rowland Phillips had a good game last Saturday, Richie Collins an even better one. But Gareth Roberts remains a more formidable flanker than Phillips. I do not want to go on about Roberts, to whom I did more than adequate justice a couple of weeks ago. What last Saturday showed was the enormous gamble which the selectors took in omitting Paul Thorburn. It came off: but it might easily have failed.

Mark Ring should have put Wales comfortably ahead with a conversion and several penalties. He missed them all and appeared as unconcerned after failing as he had been in making the original attempt. Bleddyn Bowen is no siege gun either. But he is a neat, competent little kicker: the sort of player, familiar enough to most Welsh clubs, who can dispatch the ball accurately in a lovely parabola from 35 yards. Why did he not put himself on instead of Ring, who was clearly out of sorts? This must rank as an error of captaincy comparable to Mike Harrison's decision to go for the only penalty which Jonathan Webb actually kicked, instead of pressing for a try. Webb could easily have kicked two others, one of which hit the post.

In other words, with competent kicking by England, and the incompetent kicking which Wales displayed, England would have won 12-11. If you think this analysis fanciful, remember the Scotland-France match. Scotland won deservedly 23-12. But 12 of their points were from penalties kicked by Gavin Hastings. If Hastings had been as feeble – or, if you prefer, as unlucky – as Ring, Scotland would have lost by one point.

But this, you may say, is too arithmetical an approach. Thorburn was omitted because Wales wanted to play an open, running game. That was the reason for including Anthony Clement in his place. And he did all that was asked of him, and more, even initiating Adrian Hadley's second try.

Without wishing to depreciate Clement's performance in any way, I should point out that this argument contains a fallacy. The fallacy is that if Wales play Thorburn they cannot play a running game. Throughout his career Thorburn has suffered from having 'too slow' hung around his neck. But there is no evidence either that he is too slow generally or that he is reluctant to use his speed in coming into the line.

It is said also that Clement is too good a footballer to be left out. But he is only just 21. Other Welsh stand-off halves have had to wait their turn and Clement's time will come. In the meantime, omitting Thorburn is, in the words of the Bankruptcy Act, 'a rash and hazardous speculation'.

WINGS IN, PRAYERS ANSWERED
The Independent, February 1988

I am conscious of a slightly carping note which enters these columns from time to time, and try to guard against it. It is a spirit of hyper-criticism to which Welsh rugby followers are particularly prone.

Bumping into a fellow countryman a few days ago, I asked him what he thought of last Saturday's match, expecting a response of happy enthusiasm. He looked as if he had just inspected the open coffin in the front parlour. 'I am still very worried about the Welsh back row,' he confided. 'They are still not getting the ball on the ground. They need Gareth Roberts for that.' I replied that I agreed with him. But there was a limit to the patience of readers and editors alike when it came to a bring-back-Roberts campaign, especially in view of the way things had gone for Wales so far.

Instead we should all be pleased about the season's rugby. We have seen one great match – Scotland and Wales – and at least three very good ones. We have also seen two great tries – Gavin Hastings's against France and Ieuan Evans's against Scotland – and about half a dozen excellent ones.

Moreover, wings have done quite well for once, with seven

tries altogether: two each for Adrian Hadley and Patrice Lagisquet, and one each for Iwan Tukalo, Matt Duncan and, of course, Ieuan Evans. And Hugo MacNeill's try against Scotland, scored when he came on as a substitute for Trevor Ringland, was really a winger's try also.

Alas, there is no Englishman in this list. I still think, however, that Mike Harrison was hard done by in being dropped. Against Wales he made one run in the first half which might have led to a score if he had been properly supported. Admittedly his defence is no great shakes. But then, neither is that of Gavin Hastings, on the evidence of his last match. Yet Hastings would be virtually the first name to be written into a current British Isles XV. Quite rightly, no one suggests dropping *him*.

Harrison was unlucky that all three tries against England so far were scored on his side of the field. But he is really being held responsible, with Les Cusworth and Kevin Simms, for England's failure to score any tries themselves. Certainly Chris Oti should have been brought in. But Rory Underwood is as lucky as Harrison is unlucky. Underwood's overall record is much worse. Indeed, among recent English wings holding a regular place, only Peter Squires comes below him in strike-rate, which is the ratio of tries to appearances.

These figures do not tell the full story. They depend on chances outside the players' control. In the Twickenham match, for instance, Simms ought to have passed to Underwood at least twice in the first half, when instead he passed inside on one occasion and was tackled on another. Underwood looked understandably piqued. The sad truth is, however, that he is one of those physically gifted players who nevertheless find it difficult to score tries above a certain level of the game. He is reminiscent of the schoolboy sprinter who was expected to strike alarm in the opposition, but had to be given – literally handed – the ball and then pointed in the general direction of the line. Underwood is not quite like this. But I remain unconvinced that he would have scored either of Hadley's tries, or Tukalo's try, or – above all – Evans's try.

The final table is set out as follows: wing, tries, appearances, strike-rate – appearances rather than caps because Bonneval has been capped in the centre. Only wings are counted.

	T	A	SR
Evans	6	11	0.55
Bonneval	7	14	0.50
Harrison	7	14	0.50
Duncan	7	15	0.47
Tukalo	5	11	0.45
Lagisquet	7	18	0.39
Hadley	9	24	0.38
Crossan	7	22	0.32
Ringland	9	32	0.28
Underwood	4	19	0.21
Berot	2	10	0.20

ENGLISH INJUSTICES
The Independent, March 1988

When he was at Cambridge shortly after the war, the late Hugh Lloyd-Davies commended a freshman, a flanker and a fellow Welshman, to the university captain, Eric Bole. The forward concerned was 18 or 19 at the time, he had already played for Swansea and his name was Clem Thomas.

Bole replied that no doubt he was promising, but that he was a bit young. 'If he's good enough for the Swansea pack,' Lloyd-Davies said, or words to this effect (there was one expletive which I do not reproduce), 'he's good enough for this lot.' The Cambridge captain did not take kindly to my deceased friend's forthright intervention. At any rate, Thomas's Blue was delayed for several years. Indeed, he had already played for Wales before his only appearance in the university match.

I have always taken a similar view of Jamie Salmon. Though he may not be quite such a distinguished performer in his position as Thomas used to be in his, I nevertheless feel that if he was good enough to play centre for New Zealand, he ought to be good enough for England. Last Saturday I saw him score 23 points, including two tries, for Harlequins against Waterloo, when he did enough to show that he could be the kind of calming, constructive influence which England have long needed. This is the function that Bleddyn Bowen currently fulfils for Wales.

Salmon has not been well treated by the selectors. An Englishman, he was first capped for England against New Zealand over there in June 1985 – four years after his first appearance for the All Blacks. He had a run of four matches until he was dropped after England's humiliating defeat at Murrayfield two years ago.

Among the backs, Simon Halliday and Simon Smith were dropped at the same time. In the equivalent match tomorrow, Halliday has returned; Rob Andrew and Nigel Melville are the half-backs once again after numerous permutations and flirtations; while Will Carling, also of the Quins, is preferred to Salmon. It seems a little unfair. It is more than unfair – it is ridiculous – to say that he is not among the top eight centres in England, which is the impression you gain from the divisional championship and subsequent selections.

After the Scottish match two years ago, the selectors put in Kevin Simms and Fran Clough because they were the successful Cambridge centres of the time. This pathetic explanation was about to be vouchsafed to Salmon by one of the selectors. He said he did not want to hear it; was fed up; thought he had been unjustly treated to make way for a lesser player in Clough – as indeed he had been.

Last season he was given a clear run, culminating in the Scottish match at Twickenham. This was the game in which England, after a disappointing time, surprised most people, even though the Scots did not play especially well. This was surely the team on whom to build for the present season. It would have meant retaining, among the backs, not only Salmon but also Marcus Rose and Peter Williams; among the forwards Nigel Redman, Steve Bainbridge, John Hall and Gary Rees. Melville I would have preferred to Richard Harding, because of comparative youth, Jeff Probyn to Gary Pearce because of mobility.

Instead the English selectors have allowed themselves to be swayed by the dubious evidence of the World Cup and the divisional championship. Would John Gallagher, I wonder, ever have played for England – or for Ireland – if he had stayed in south London instead of going to New Zealand?

FOCUS ON THE FAST FORWARDS
The Independent, March 1988

At the beginning of the week, I was cranking myself up for a grand assault on the BBC. Viewers in England, I assumed, would be shown the whole of the Irish game, where the only remotely interesting question would be whether the home side would be able to score a try. They would then have to content themselves with an edited version of the French match in Cardiff.

Well, for once the Corporation is doing the right thing, showing Wales's Grand Slam game against France live, and the complete match from Twickenham afterwards. This amounts to three hours of continuous rugby, the maximum period my video recorder can digest.

Never underestimate technology. Just as it will change – is already changing – the nature of journalism, so also the video recorder is changing the way in which we look at sport. Provided he knows the laws (or the rules as we call them in Wales), the ordinary follower of the game can challenge both referee and television commentator. Nor is the recording machine a totally beneficial invention from the point of view of those journalists who are covering a match. It means that their reports can be challenged subsequently. It is, according to the way you look at these things, an extension of sporting knowledge and democracy, or yet another encroachment on respect for properly constituted authority.

For myself, I belong to the first, or democratic, school. Let there be light is what I say – or, anyway, action replays. We all know that referees have to make up their minds on the spot.

If they are wrong, it does not mean they are no good. But it does not mean, either, that we have to keep quiet about their mistakes. Here are some reflections on the season so far.

One of the most obvious aspects is the failure to spot – or it may be the toleration of – the forward pass. On my count, the majority of tries scored after a movement have followed such passes. Adrian Hadley's first try against England came after an initial forward pass by Richie Collins. Ieuan Evans's great try against Scotland was set up by a forward pass. At least one of Patrice Lagisquet's tries against Ireland was faulty in the same respect.

Of course, it is nice to see wings scoring tries, even though the supply rather dried up last Saturday. It is pleasant to see three-quarter movements at all. Understandably, referees are reluctant to spoil a flow on those rare occasions when there is one. But the law is the law. The referee has no discretion about enforcing it in this area, as he does in others. He has a discretion, for instance, about what constitutes a readjustment. Yet almost invariably here the decision goes against the player. Likewise, any failure to catch the ball cleanly is liable to be judged a knock-on, irrespective of where the ball lands. Jonathan Webb suffered in this way against France, when the ball hit the ground fractionally behind vertical.

The more serious infringements, however, which referees have consistently failed to spot, have lain in the field of obstruction and of being in an offside position while interfering with play, though pretending not to be doing anything of the kind. David Frost had a most interesting article in Another Newspaper earlier in the week in which he demonstrated how the Scottish forwards last Saturday, trying to ruck *à la* New Zealand, missed or went over the ball and ended up offside but unpenalised.

Nor are they alone. Phil May tends to shoot out of the lineouts on his opponents' side for no other purpose than to disrupt their possession, if they secure any. On these occasions, he makes no attempt to catch the ball himself or to protect Wales's possession. It is purely – or, rather, impurely – a spoiling operation. He then puts his hands innocently above his head, like a terrorist trying vainly to surrender to the SAS.

Jeff Probyn's somewhat different activities deserve and will receive a column all to themselves some day. For the moment, I conclude with an exchange between the former Irish prop, Mike Fitzpatrick, and a referee: 'You're boring, Fitzpatrick.' 'You're none too entertaining yourself, Ref.'

OLD TIMES AT CARDIFF
The Independent, March 1988

When I first visited the Cardiff Arms Park in 1946 I was 12, I had seen nothing of the world east of Swansea or north of Aberystwyth, and my expectations were not high. Even so, the ground struck me as squalid. It seemed to be constructed – and not very well constructed – of rusting corrugated iron and rotting wood. The prevailing smell was of urine.

St Helen's, Swansea (where internationals continued to be played until 1954), was to me an altogether more stylish location. With its single large stand, its handsome cricket pavilion and its view of Swansea Bay, which, so we were informed by our elders with unfailing and tedious regularity, was at least the equal and maybe the superior of the Bay of Naples. This was where I had watched my previous internationals, which had been service affairs. These matches, and the other inter-service contests of the war years, made up the best rugby I ever saw.

After all, Wales could turn out Flying Officer B. L. Williams, Sergeant W. T. H. Davies, Lieutenant H. Tanner and Captain A. J. Risman; while England, stronger in the pack, boasted Squadron Leaders R. H. G. Weighill and H. B. Toft, Corporal J. Mycock and Sergeant G. T. Dancer (a Lion in 1938 who never won a full cap). It was the presence of Rugby League players which made these matches memorable – and not only Risman, even though he was the greatest of them all, whether from League or Union. This is the reason for my wish to see the two codes come together at the highest levels, and not merely those of amateur players, members of the armed services and inmates of HM prisons. How, I sometimes wonder, would Bath fare against Widnes under Union rules? (As Widnes would have to find two extra men there might even be a place at flanker for Jonathan Davies.)

These matches were followed by the Victory Internationals, for which no full caps were awarded. As club rugby had restarted in 1945 I still do not see why full internationals could not have been resumed in the following year. Hugh Lloyd-Davies always resented not receiving a full cap for his appearances in the Victory Internationals. Though barely in his 20s, he never played full-back for Wales again. He used to excoriate the Welsh selectors for their timidity in preferring the safer but less exciting Frank Trott of Cardiff. But in the England game Dicky Guest went round him twice to win the match, so I could see their point of view. In fact, they had turned first to the pre-war international Howard Davies of Llanelli, who played in all four matches of the 1947 season.

He was the full-back in the first recognised international that I saw at the Arms Park. In front of him he had Ken Jones, Jack Matthews, Billy Cleaver and Les Williams, with Haydn Tanner at scrum-half and – the cause of fierce controversy – Bleddyn Williams at outside-half for the first time. It was the last time too. Though Wales scored two unconverted tries, from Rees Stephens and Gwyn Evans, England won 9-6 with a converted try from Don White and a dropped goal from the late Nim Hall, who looked at death's door even as a young man but who nevertheless always seemed to be dropping goals. He dropped one again at Cardiff in 1949, but England lost 9-3 after two marvellous wing's tries from Les Williams and a try by the forward Alan Meredith. Still, Wales ended the season with the wooden spoon.

As you can see, the goal-kicking was not up to much in those days, unless the Cardiff policeman Ewart Tamplin was in the side. That, at any rate, is one department in which Wales have improved. Indeed, I expect Paul Thorburn's boot to win tomorrow's match.

NOT JUST A MATTER OF DESERTS

The Independent, March 1988

I was reading a piece in Another Newspaper the other day in which the writer was arguing that Wales did not deserve to win the Grand Slam in Cardiff tomorrow – or even that share in the championship which they are now bound to obtain. (If they draw they win the championship outright but not, of course, the Grand Slam, which requires four straight wins.) This question of deserts is quite a tricky one. There are numerous solid citizens who do not believe that Mrs Margaret Thatcher deserved to win the last election. There are times when we have to accept things as they are and make the best of them.

Four years ago, for instance, I did not believe that Jim Aitken's Scotland deserved to win the Grand Slam. They seemed a pretty average lot to me. I wrote as much in a magazine. A titled Scottish lady complained to the editor, a friend of hers. As I had gone on at tedious length for months, she said, about Swansea and Llanelli – teams in whom she had as little interest as I in Hawick and Gala – why could I not show some generosity to the Scots when they managed to pull off something? It later turned out that she was in love with Andy Irvine. Nevertheless, she had a point, irrespective of her motives. We should try to show some generosity.

We all know that Wales still possess faults. They still need a proper No 8, though Dean Richards remains the only Lion-standard player in that position in the home countries. The back row were outpaced by the Scots. Wales continued to rely overmuch on Robert Norster, who will not be fully fit tomorrow even though he will be playing.

But several other doubts which existed at the beginning of the season were dissipated. The front row proved solid. Jeff Probyn, he of the ferocious reputation, made not the slightest dent on Staff Jones, who returns tomorrow. Among the backs, Robert Jones settled the David Bishop argument, for another season at least. Paul Thorburn demonstrated that he could run as well as kick, which some of us had known anyway. And Adrian Hadley finally put to rest those doubts about his speed and his alertness.

It is not widely realised that Hadley, at only 25, is a highly experienced player. He was first capped in 1983, as were Mark Ring and Bleddyn Bowen also. Thorburn and Jonathan Davies played first for Wales in 1985, Jones in 1986. Only Ieuan Evans, who won his first cap against France last season, is a comparative newcomer. Yet people persist in writing about the Welsh backs as if they have just arrived on the scene. What is true is that they have played, or been encouraged to play, more freely. They have already done enough to deserve a Grand Slam. In entertainment value, most observers would agree with the following order: 1 Wales; 2 France; 3 Scotland; 4 Ireland; 5 England.

At the beginning of the season, I put £100 on France to win the championship at 2-1 on. I have friends who think this an unpatriotic or disloyal thing to do, to bet against your native land. I disagree. But it serves me right. If Wales win or draw, bang goes £100. If France win, however, and so share the championship, I do not get back £50. I do not even receive £25, for a half-share in the championship.

Oh no. What I perhaps somewhat grandly call my bookmakers inform me that, in the circumstances, I owe them £25. The £100 bet is split into two bets of £50. One I lose, so owing them £50. The other I win, so being owed £25. Accordingly, I owe *them* the balance of £25. No wonder there are no poor bookmakers.

BOARD WALK ON THIN ICE

The Independent, April 1988

A senior Minister, much concerned with the forthcoming invitation tour of South Africa, was expressing puzzlement a few days ago. Why, he asked me, had the International Board suddenly placed their seal of approval on the projected visit? What had changed? Life had certainly been made slightly more difficult for him on this account. All I could suggest was that it seemed a good idea at the time. I was somewhat ashamed of the feebleness of my answer, and apologised to my ministerial interlocutor. But it appears that I was broadly right.

The remarks of John Kendall-Carpenter of the IB are most curious. The tour, he laments, has all of a sudden assumed what he calls 'a high profile'. What on earth did he expect, in all the circumstances? It was not as if he and his colleagues had just given their approval to the Kendall-Carpenter All Stars Invitation XV to play Brynamman on the occasion of their centenary celebrations. Obviously there was going to be a row involving, among other forthcoming attractions, the Seoul Olympics and the Cardiff Commonwealth Games.

Let us return to the senior Minister. He wishes the board had not bestowed their imprimatur. He stands by the Gleneagles agreement, which laid down that signatory countries would use their best endeavours to discourage their nationals from playing in or against South Africa. Accordingly, he will echo Margaret Thatcher at Question Time on Tuesday and urge the players who may be invited not to go. He approves of the attitude taken by the English authorities – even though England were in 1984 the last European country to play South Africa. Further than this, the Minister is not prepared to go. Exhortation is all. Is this true liberalism? Or false liberalism? Or plain humbug?

There is no doubt that the government could take action if it wished. It could deprive players accepting invitations of their passports as they were about to make the outward journey. The issue or withdrawal of a passport is a purely executive act. No appeal to the law courts is possible. This is, in my opinion, a scandal. There should be a right to a passport, unless due cause is shown. It should be withdrawn only by a court. But that, alas, is not the present position.

The home unions could also take action. They could announce that players accepting invitations would be deemed to have disbarred themselves from further consideration for national selection. The unions would be most unlikely to take this course. For one thing, they would be depriving themselves of their better players. For another, they might be laying themselves open to legal action. A few years ago, the cricket authorities thought they could discipline the Packer defectors. They were smartly called to order by Mr Justice (now Lord Justice) Slade. Admittedly, considerations of contract and restraint of trade were involved there as they are not involved here. But I should not bank on the unions' untrammelled power.

Lastly, employers could take action, as they have done in the past. Teachers and policemen working for Labour local authorities are particularly at risk, not only in Wales but elsewhere. John Carleton relinquished his job as a teacher in Lancashire and adopted another following his Lions visit in 1980.

I hope none of these sanctions is employed. For once, I am on the government's side. Moreover, I do not even presume to advise players to refuse any invitation that may be proffered. It is up to them. Phil Bennett, apropos the 1974 Lions tour of South Africa, said that he would play rugby anywhere, against anyone. He would play on the moon, if necessary. That was typical west Wales hyperbole. But it was nonetheless a noble sentiment.

There are those who believe that the South African political regime is uniquely wicked. I agree that it is wicked. But in the scale I should place the Khmer Rouge in Cambodia, or Hitler in Germany, below it. That, however, is not the point. The point is that rugby should assert its independence. As Lincoln said of the disasters that might ensue from the American Civil War: 'Let the grass grow where it may.'

RAISING THE CLASS BARRIERS
The Independent, April 1988

The rise and fall of empires, or of civilisations, used to be a favourite subject for historians, and now seems to be coming back into academic fashion. Rugby clubs rise and fall in the same way. Here are some preliminary generalisations, supported by examples.

It is harder to rise than it is to fall. Until quite recently (by which I mean the last 20 years or so) virtually the only English club who had attained first class status by breaking through a barrier were Wasps. Saracens were an in-between sort of case, as indeed they still are. High hopes used to be reposed in Esher and in Streatham-Croydon, not least because of the consistently entertaining performance of the latter club in the Middlesex Sevens. But these hopes were disappointed.

Outside London the prospects of breaking through have turned out to be more encouraging. The last couple of decades have seen at least two clubs attain first class status: Orrell and Nottingham. The latest club on the edge of success is the newly merged Liverpool St Helens.

There is, however, a distinction to be drawn between great clubs and first class clubs. Leicester and Wasps used to be first class clubs but have become great only in the last few years. Blackheath used to be a great club but are now merely first class – if that. Richmond are a similar, though less clear-cut case, though I personally shall always consider them great.

London Scottish have long been a great club and they still are, just about. London Irish have never been great, though they have made up for it in niceness and general sociability. London Welsh (it is often forgotten) used to be much like London Irish, if not more so, until the likes of Roger Michaelson and John Dawes transformed them into a great club in the mid-to-late 1960s. Are the Welsh still a great club? They are certainly not a great *side* any longer. But greatness, once attained, is a quality that is difficult to lose altogether. Cardiff, Swansea and Llanelli from Wales, Harlequins, Bath and Bristol from England, will – I like to think – be great clubs whatever happens in terms of playing results.

Yet, nevertheless, greatness can be lost: look at Blackheath. In the 1920s and 1930s some of the old boys and hospital clubs were numbered among the greats. Today they are not considered even first class. The same applies to the services. All the Welsh valley clubs have declined, except Pontypool, who have become great only recently, comparatively speaking.

After the last war the leading clubs were Cardiff, Coventry

and Oxford University. None of them have enjoyed a successful season but they are still considered great clubs, with a question mark against Coventry. In the last decade and more an effort has been made by some commentators to deprive Oxford and Cambridge of their claim to greatness, or even of first class status. The hearties (such as Wilfred Wooller) and the surly anti-élitists (no names, no writs) have combined to say that we take the ancient universities too seriously. The hearties complain about the imposition of academic standards and the consequent weakening of university sport; the anti-élitists are merely embittered about the existence of Oxford and Cambridge at all.

All these judgements used to be based not only on great players produced, spectacular results achieved, but also on sentiment and tradition. This season has seen a great change, with the introduction of the leagues. They will alter the way in which we evaluate clubs. In the final judgement, however, sentiment and tradition will still be the arbiter. Sale, Waterloo and even Richmond will always be great clubs to me. And I shall never be able to take Rosslyn Park, Orrell and Liverpool St Helens wholly seriously, whatever the tables may say.

QUINS A CAPITAL SUCCESS
The Independent, April 1988

London clubs have appeared in the last three finals of the John Player Cup, London Welsh three years ago, Wasps on the two subsequent occasions. Every time they lost to Bath, the club that no one likes very much, apart from their own ill-behaved supporters.

This year the play remains the same, with a West Country club facing one from London. But the cast changes. I hope that prince among Press officers, John Gasson of Wasps, will not be offended if I say that I am glad that it is Harlequins who are taking on Bristol. Though I have spent several entertaining and instructive afternoons at Sudbury over the past few seasons, it is pleasant to have a change. And Quins, in the new year, have provided – with no ifs, buts or qualifications – the best rugby I have witnessed from an English club. In the past few months they have run Waterloo off the Stoop and reduced Nottingham to the level of a pensioned-off cart-horse. Perhaps Stoop brings out the best in them, though the ground does not suit spectators nearly so well. The pitch is so far away from the small stand that you feel almost as if you are at a race-meeting, requiring sharp eyes or field glasses to have much idea of what is going on.

But it did not need spectacles of any kind to confirm, in the Nottingham match, that Andrew Harriman, another black wing, was faster than Chris Oti, even though Oti was not playing for Nottingham on this occasion. In September 1986, against Leicester, Harriman twice demonstrated that he was faster than Rory Underwood in a more directly convincing manner. Once he caught Underwood from behind and once he outstripped him, though he failed to score, being forced into touch by another player. For this match, Harriman was the third choice on the Quins right wing. Even today he is only the second choice, with Jon Eagle as the first preference.

Harlequins possess extraordinary strength in depth, and are able also to prefer Stuart Thresher to Marcus Rose, Will Carling to Charles Smith, Everton Davis to Simon Hunter, Richard Moon to Alex Woodhouse, Paul Curtis to David Butcher and, it may well be when the final comes, Adrian Thompson to the new Scottish international Richard Cramb. Thompson was originally a centre, fast, elusive and wiry, but was probably too slight for the position. As a press-ganged stand-off, his great merit is that he cannot kick. This means that either he has a go himself or he passes the ball, to the general increase in public pleasure – and, it must be said, to the advantage of his own side.

The decisions have been taken, the choices made, by Jamie Salmon, even though his two caps for New Zealand in 1981 were as a centre rather than as a second five-eighths. His playing in the last few months has been virtually perfect. How England feel able to do without him I cannot understand. From observing the young man, I guess that he displays insufficient deference towards the powers that be. Indeed, a Lions pairing of Salmon and Mark Ring would not appear far-fetched.

Another New Zealand product, Dirk Williams, strengthened the back row considerably, though Tim Bell (a wing converted to No 7) is an excellent substitute of the nippier, more old-fashioned kind. Whether Williams will be allowed to play in the final remains to be seen.

If anyone is to be picked out, however, I should choose the young lock, Neil Edwards, coupled with the captain, John Olver. They have all shown that you do not have to confine yourself to 10- or nine-man rugby to win matches.

A GOOD SEASON
The Independent, April 1988

It has been one of the best season for years. The Courage Clubs championship has turned out to be a greater success than expected, marred mainly by a silly points system whereby clubs are rewarded merely for turning up. The Five Nations championship saw several great matches and even more fine tries, with wings at last being given a chance to function as something other than additional full-backs. The luckiest country were France, who could easily have gone down to England and Wales, as well as to Scotland. The ill-luck was spread fairly evenly among the home countries: each might have won at least one match which they in fact lost.

There were two collective achievements, apart from individual feats. One was by the Welsh backs, who often played as if they were Barbarians of old at Swansea on Easter Monday (alas, a fixture that is now sadly diminished). The other achievement was by the English forwards, whose formidable play in the loose showed the influence of Roger Uttley. There are colleagues who consider that England were unwise to bring in Uttley when it was known he could not accompany the side to Australia. I disagree. Coaches such as Alan Jones and the late Carwyn James have done wonders with club (especially university) sides over a shortish period. There is no reason why national teams should not benefit similarly.

It was not all happy enthusiasm. The county championship aroused even less interest than usual. Indeed, on the day of the final I took myself off to Old Deer Park to see Wasps defeat London Welsh. Nor did the divisional championship sound the blast of the trumpet but, rather, the peep of the tin whistle. The only good thing about it was that it was over before Christmas. My solution is to hold it at the same time of year but to cease pretending that it has anything to do with English national selection and to open it to club players who are qualified to appear for Scotland, Wales or Ireland.

The trouble with the season is that it has been effectively over since the middle of March, when Wales shared the championship with France. For weeks we have known that Leicester would, deservedly, win the league. In England, the sole topic of interest for virtually the whole of this month has been whether Bristol or Harlequins would win the John Player Cup tomorrow.

There is no need for the season to end on this note of anti-climax. The fifth and final round of internationals should be held not in March but in April. This would be followed, on the second or third Saturday, by the John Player Cup. And, on the fourth Saturday, the league champions would play the Barbarians, which might do something to revive that old club.

ENGLAND OVERPRAISED
The Independent, October 1988

My own impressions of the season so far differ slightly from those of some other observers. When it began, the success of the English senior clubs against the Welsh – on the first full

Saturday they had a clean sweep – led some people to say that the English players were fitter, the leagues were paying off, Wales must introduce a similar system or perish, and anyway Welsh rugby was in a terrible mess: just look at the number of players going north. All this may have been true enough up to a point, but the conclusion that was drawn was clearly wrong. This was that English rugby must therefore be in a promising condition. On the contrary: all the faults that were apparent in the national side last season have been on display in club sides this season. Some of these failings have been compounded by the league system itself, with the emphasis on percentage rugby.

Almost everyone agrees that the leagues have been a success. They have aroused interest and enthusiasm where neither existed before. I do not, I confess, greatly look forward to the prospect of London Welsh's descent into the Third Division, where they will be playing clubs such as Maidstone. I have nothing against Maidstone, but I still retain some loyalty. This kind of demotion is part of the fun, if you like to think of it in that way. The matches themselves, however, seem to be less fun than they were last season. Then we had a crazy points system where you got marks just for turning up. Now the scoring system is two points for a win, one for a draw. It might help to make the change which the Football League introduced a few years ago, and award three points for a win. I write 'might' because, from my own perfunctory observations, this change did not lead to livelier soccer. I am not dogmatic about these things, but three points for a win, one for a draw, could be tried out next season.

It is difficult to say why this dourness has come into English rugby at club, as distinct from international, level. Harlequins, last season, showed that it was possible to perform respectably in the league and to win the Cup by playing always attractive and sometimes spectacular football. Today Quins still try to play the same kind of game, even though their encounter with Wasps a couple of weeks ago was a pretty grim affair. But the trouble is that, in other matches, their attempts at open rugby have not come off.

Their coach, Dick Best, is in charge of London for the

match against Australia tomorrow. His own club provide just under half the side and it will be instructive to note the extent to which Best has transferred the characteristics of Quins to the division. Some of Best's hallmarks are worth the transfer – for instance, the disinclination to mess around when the ball is coming out of the scrum on your own side. Profitlessly holding the ball in the back row has been the curse of English rugby for years.

Other Harlequins characteristics are less admirable – for instance, the elevation of the tapped penalty into an article of dogma. There is seldom a case for preferring a speculative four or six points to a probable three. But this is not the kind of mistake which I expect to see London make. I shall be backing them if Mr Ladbroke can give the right odds.

POPULAR GAME OF NATIONAL IDENTITY
The Independent, October 1988

If my colleagues are to be believed, we may see some Anglo-Welsh cross-fertilisation in the international championship this season. Colin Laity, who comes from Cornwall and plays for Neath, could be chosen by Wales; while Dewi Morris, who comes from Breconshire and plays for Liverpool St Helens, could be chosen by England. I think Morris is the likelier bet for a cap, partly because scrum-halves are in shorter supply in England than centres are in Wales, and partly because the English selectors have traditionally been more, shall we say, flexible about national qualifications than have the Welsh selectors about their own national side.

However, if I were an English selector (which thank the Lord I'm not, sir) I should be inclined to go not for a fully paid-up Welshman in Morris but for a half-Welshman in Steve Bates of Wasps. He was brought up in London but his father comes from Merthyr. I was about to write that he had been 'in the shadow' of Nigel Melville for a long time. But, as poor old Melville has been injured so often and so seriously,

Bates has effectively been the Wasps' first choice at scrum-half for several seasons now. As such he has been an excellently unobtrusive operator who rarely takes a wrong option. He certainly deserves a chance at the highest level.

On the whole, I approve of the tolerance and eclecticism of the English selectors. It was nevertheless, I used to think, a little unfair when the English teams of the post-war period contained a procession of South African Rhodes scholars from Oxford. It was even more unfair when Scotland chose Doug Keller in 1949, who was to win seven caps after having been in the Australian touring team of 1947. Jamie Salmon, on the other hand, is clearly English. The wonder with him is that it took the selectors so long to appreciate him.

The Welsh selectors, by contrast, gain something and lose more by their narrow nationalism. They seem to think that rugby begins at Llanelli and ends at Newport. What they gain in cohesion they lose in talent. True, some choices have been distinctly on the far-flung side, though Ian Jones, who won a single cap 20 years ago, was a South African of Welsh ancestry on both sides. I always had my doubts about the provenance of Mike Roberts. And John Taylor could easily have played for England.

The general rule is, however, that where there is an option, Welsh players opt for England, while English players – Laity is exceptional – do not opt for Wales. Recent English internationals who could have opted for Wales include Stuart Barnes, Will Carling, Gareth Chilcott, Huw Davies, Simon Halliday (born in Haverfordwest) and Nigel Redman (born in Cardiff). Of these, the most useful addition to the Welsh side would perhaps have been Redman. For several seasons now the Welsh second row has consisted of Robert Norster and A. N. Other.

The problem does not look like going away. Indeed, it will be exacerbated when Norster finally takes his leave. But Redman made the wise choice: he would have been unlikely to be chosen by the parochial Welsh. Not only do they neglect players such as Redman. They also refuse to consider what one might call 'true Welshmen' who have emigrated to English clubs, such as Bleddyn Jones, formerly of Leicester. It used to be the case that, in London, only London Welsh players were considered for the national side. No longer, it seems: Mark Douglas has been shamefully disregarded ever since he joined London Welsh from Llanelli. Dewi Morris has manifestly made the wise choice.

WASPS' LIGHT BLUE STING
The Observer, October 1988

Though Wasps and Rosslyn Park have been playing each other for years, their encounters have usually been as enthusiastically received as a wet Sunday in Sudbury. No longer. The league has managed to raise the spirits even of the supporters of London clubs. It is not just one hand clapping while two dogs disport themselves on the touchline.

The effect on the players is more ambiguous. The Wasps and Rosslyn Park packs started off with as much niggle and bad temper as two Welsh clubs in February. Gradually the players seemed to decide to play football. The first half was remarkable. After 30 minutes Park found themselves 16 points up, probably to their surprise as much as anyone's.

There was a general pattern to all these scores. Wasps would gain possession, usually somewhat untidily, it must be said. Huw Davies would then come into the line, exhibiting considerable pace and elusiveness. After beating a few Park players, he would pass the ball, whereupon either the pass would be intercepted or the ball would go to ground, to be picked up by a Park player who would run 50 yards and score. Obviously this kind of nonsense could not go on – or so the black-blazered Wasps committeemen said hopefully in the tiny little stand. It took a boot by Foulds of Park to restore those hopes. Mr Trigg spotted it, Rob Andrew took the penalty – he missed only two kicks during the afternoon – Davies inevitably scored the first Wasps try and Andrew converted. From that moment, Park never looked like retaining their lead.

In the second half, the Cambridge/North London axis

184

became dominant, with tries from Andrew, Simon Smith and Ellison, and a cross-kick by Andrew from which the non-Cantabrigian young wing Pilgrim scored in the corner.

As far as this season's England prospects go, Davies (unless he is too old to be a prospect) was as quick as ever, Andrew kicked well, Rendall trundled around courageously with a sore throat, while Probyn – the drop-head prop – trundled around equally bravely with a dead leg. Wasps' outstanding forward, however, was Rigby, normally a blind-side rather than an open-side flanker, as he was on this occasion.

THE DAYS OF MINI-MAGIC

The Independent, October 1988

Our own brand of mini-rugby, as played in Tycroes, Carmarthenshire, over 40 years ago (and as it was played in neighbouring villages too), differed in certain respects from the version now approved by the authorities.

We sometimes played it with a soccer or even a tennis ball if there was no rugby ball to hand. If, however, a soccer ball was the only sort available, a brisk preliminary debate would take place as to the code to follow. Sometimes soccer won, sometimes rugby, depending largely on which recent international match was fresh in our young minds. But usually there was no difficulty about getting hold of the right ball: a massive, laced, ankle-breaking piece of hand-stitched leatherwork, inflated with a bicycle-pump and quite unlike the lightweight jobs now used in the game. (Children or their parents can also now buy smaller, plastic balls at Woolworth's

– a great advance since my day.) The standard of kit varied, from a reasonable approximation to the real thing – though no one had proper rugby shorts, with pockets – to ordinary clothes, minus coat and pullover.

We did not play along the '25' and across the pitch, which is what present-day exponents of mini-rugby do. Instead, we used a quarter of the full pitch, giving us a playing area of 55 by 38-odd yards. The reason was that the ground sloped crosswise, from one touchline to the other, so we selected the flattest quarter. No one watched us, apart from the occasional couple of locals, equipped with shotguns and followed by greyhounds, breaking their journey to the woods. They would make genial but derisive comments and pass on to their shooting. How different it is at Old Deer Park, at the games which Mr Neil Kinnock used to supervise. I once heard, I swear I did, a young-to-middle-aged man shout at his bemused offspring: 'For God's sake get your retaliation in first, Seamus.' Cries of 'Kill him' addressed to uniformly kitted-out little boys are not uncommon – the parents being infinitely more savage than the tiny players.

We were not soft in our day, mind you. We were not in the business of playing touch rugby, except on the road or in the school playground. All the laws of the adult game were observed. They were enforced by consent. Sometimes a member of the village club, having completed what was laughingly called 'training' (running twice round the pitch and then practising goal-kicking), would take charge of the proceedings. But this was exceptional. We could, I suppose, have press-ganged one of ourselves into refereeing. In fact, if an odd number turned up, we played seven against six, six against five, or whatever it happened to be.

We did not scrummage. We were, however, very keen on recognised positions, as they allowed us to play at being Bleddyn Williams, Haydn Tanner or Ken Jones, though there were no takers for Dr Jack Matthews. Accordingly, a team of seven would consist of full-back, right-wing, centre, left-wing, stand-off half, scrum-half and forward. The forwards, one for each side, would go down with heads touching, feet apart, hands on knees. The scrum-half would feed the ball between them and it became a simple test of quickness of reaction.

We then formed a youth team, quite independently of the senior club, to play 15-a-side rugby. I have a photograph to prove it. As I was considered to be more agile with a pen than on the pitch, I was appointed honorary secretary, while retaining my place on the right wing. Neither as fast as Ken Jones nor as elusive as Dicky Guest, I used to adopt a bull-at-the-gate approach and modelled myself on T. G. H. Jackson of Scotland. In 1948, when we were due to play a match against Cefneithin, only the late Carwyn James turned up – and he was clearly too old to play youth rugby in that year. We were most successful. It would be nice to report that we produced numerous internationals. In fact, one of us went on to play full-back briefly for Swansea. But we had a good time. And we organised it for ourselves.

ENGLAND TEETER ON SEE-SAW
The Independent, November 1988

Six times a week since the season began, and twice on Sundays, I have been reading that English rugby has improved in an extraordinary fashion. As a corollary, I have been told that Welsh rugby has declined catastrophically. We, particularly journalists, are so constructed mentally that we are always using the metaphor of the pair of scales or the see-saw. If one country is up, the other must be down. So, if England have risen, Wales must have fallen. This is not only illogical – for both countries could have either improved or declined simultaneously. It also does not accord with the facts as I have observed them. But it is fairly easy to see how the misunderstanding has come about.

The English divisional sides have defeated an unexpectedly weak Australian side. Paradoxically, perhaps the most highly regarded English coach, Alan Davies, failed to beat them, both with his 'B' team and with his Midlands Division. On the first occasion he had to contend not only with his opponents but also with the selectors. This is a not uncommon situation for a coach to be in. On the second occasion he was beaten quite fairly, the referee being correct to penalise those of his players who fell over the ball. On both occasions he would have been better advised to observe a period of silence afterwards.

However, the question we should be asking is not why English rugby has gone up, if it has, but why Australian rugby has gone down. Perhaps the decline illustrates no more than (I write in the rugby sense only) the late Alan Jones's dictum that at one minute you may be cock of the walk and at the next a feather duster.

But has English rugby come up in any significant way? Another part of the explanation for the misunderstanding lies in the league system. The crowds are up. The excitement is high. Indeed, non-league Saturdays are now entirely different in atmosphere from league Saturdays. But is the rugby any better on the latter occasions? It is certainly more serious in purpose. Sometimes good matches result, such as the recent one between Wasps and Rosslyn Park.

Nevertheless, all the old faults are still present. There is too much messing about at the back of the scrum, with a consequential slow release of the ball. The stand-off half or the inside-centre still runs back into his forwards for no discernible purpose at all. This season's fashionable move is the overhead pass which misses not one man but two, being intended for the player on the outside, usually though not invariably the wing. What happens, nine times out of 10, is that the ball lands well behind the chap for whom it was meant. It is then either booted desperately into touch or secured by the other side.

As a disinterested observer, I do not greatly care whether I am proved right or wrong at Twickenham tomorrow. I should like to be proved wrong for the sake of a good game. Andrew Harriman and Dewi Morris are adventurous choices. Neil Edwards would have been a more adventurous choice than his older fellow Harlequin Paul Ackford. Andy Robinson deserves his place on form. About David Egerton at

No 6 I am more doubtful. I was more worried still when, on *Rugby Special*, Geoff Cooke gave the reason for his selection. This was that, in Cooke's phrase, the 'work-rate' of the regular blind-side flankers whom the selectors had inspected had not proved satisfactory. If work-rate is what Cooke is after, what is wrong with John Wells of Leicester? But the truth, I am afraid, is that the phrase (redolent of Sir Alf Ramsey) would never be used at all by anyone with a real desire to play open rugby. It is the kind of phrase that betrays its user. I hope I am proved wrong tomorrow.

TELEVISION MUST BE NURSE TO REBIRTH
The Independent, November 1988

Everyone I have spoken to this week has said: 'What a marvellous match,' or words to that effect. Admittedly, I have not spoken to any Australians. But Welshmen, Scotsmen and Irishmen all hope that England will carry on playing as they did last Saturday, even if it means that their own national sides are defeated as the Australians were. There is certainly a lot of goodwill around. There is even talk of a rugby renaissance. Whether it turns out to be justified depends rather on the way New Zealand are regarded. They can be looked on either as ordinary competitors or as superior beings. If they are viewed in the latter way, we can improve no end and still not be expected to beat them.

But, if rugby is improving as we are told it is, should not television be doing more to assist the process? Should it not be doing more in any event? International matches, admittedly, are covered more comprehensively and more interestingly every year. There were seven cameras at Twickenham last Saturday, a record. I should like to hear more sound-effects – lineout calls and even half-time talks – as we did in the broadcasts of the World Cup. There are powerful arguments against such an extension: notably that words are often spoken which are better left unrecorded; that these are private occasions for the players; and the spectators at the ground do not hear these instructions or exchanges. The solution may lie in providing edited versions only.

Rugby Special has improved greatly over the past couple of seasons. It would be churlish to deny it. Nevertheless, we still have the likes of Hawick v Gala shoved in at the middle or towards the end. Why we have to be shown these games, when the Scots already have their own programme, I do not know. Nor do some of the people connected with the programme. Chris Rea is, however, an excellent presenter and interviewer, even though – or perhaps because – he reminds me of the Edinburgh lady who, at a performance of *Swan Lake*, said it was no doubt very pretty, but a bit exaggerated. The other change is that the programme is on at the regular time of 5.05 p.m., something on which the Rugby Union insisted. At the moment the programme is trying to strike the right balance between edited extracts, interviews and comment. Last season, there was even a somewhat eccentric instructional series featuring a middle-aged coach, a small boy and a young woman from Loughborough. I look forward to her return, at any rate.

There is no reason why the programme should not look at rugby in a variety of ways. It was, after all, what we were demanding several seasons ago. My feeling is, however, that it is now trying to cram too much into the time available. Last Sunday there was a strong case for devoting the entire show to the Australian match (not only extracts, but interviews and comment), while leaving the French match for more leisurely consideration. Why not a programme on the state of French rugby? It would be at least as interesting as Hawick v Gala. And why, for that matter, need it be made by the BBC?

Some time ago I wrote that rugby was not covered by ITV in England, as distinct from Wales. I received a courteous letter of correction from the novelist and broadcaster, Derek Robinson. Rugby, he wrote, was indeed covered by ITV in the West Country. The tragedy is that Channel 4 refused to have anything to do with rugby. Its first chief, Jeremy Isaacs, said he would cover only obscure or minority sports, and gave us American football. But he also gave us the widely admired *Channel 4 Racing*. We should have *Channel 4 Rugby* too.

LONDON WELSH
The Independent, December 1988

The London Welsh club have virtually decided to become open, or go public. The principal reason given for the change is that the cost of living in London is now so high that young men no longer cross the border so readily as they did, say, 20 years ago, at the beginning of the club's great period. Though I have every sympathy with young people who are trying to buy a house – the price of houses in London is now very silly – the argument does not entirely convince me. Why, if it is valid, should the other 'exile' clubs be flourishing as they appear to be doing? There is no sound from Sunbury that London Irish are considering going public, or from the Welsh's neighbours London Scottish.

It has been suggested that the Irish have a better 'support system' than the Welsh; that whereas the Welsh's principal non-playing club members tend to be teachers or other worthy folk without much money, the Irish have an endless supply of rich builders who can provide houses and jobs for players. It is said also that the Scots who come down to London find well-paid jobs. But for every Gavin Hastings (though I have no idea what he is paid in his surveyor's office) there is someone like George Graham, the army corporal, who is, incidentally, the most mobile prop I have seen since the late Cliff Davies was playing.

Though there may be something in these explanations, they have always been valid, more or less. The truth is that London Welsh are going through a bad patch, as all clubs do, sooner or later. Pontypool are not the force they were, Harlequins have been disappointing this season (at any rate in terms of results), while Wasps have not always met their own high standards. The difference is, of course, that the last two of these clubs are in the English First Division, and look as if they will stay there. The Welsh are at the bottom of the Second, and look certain to descend to the Third. It is this which has concentrated the minds of the authorities at Old Deer Park. For, as long as the Welsh could secure the occasional spectacular and unexpected home win over, say, Llanelli or Bridgend (as they managed in recent seasons), so long could they delude themselves that they remained a truly first class club.

There is another factor. The great days of the late 1960s and the early 1970s have led to a misreading of the club's history. Those years were an aberrantly successful period. For most of their history the club have been content to paddle along somewhere near the top of the Second Division. But during that time, First and Second Divisions were matters of reputation rather than of calculation; they were in the mind, rather than in printed tables. Indeed, if the Welsh do go public, this will be the first major effect of the new league system. John Taylor is against this change. So is another survivor of the great era, Ian Jones.

By the way, I was wrong to suggest that Jones, having been brought up in South Africa, was unqualified to play for Wales. His paternal grandparents emigrated from west Wales at the end of the 19th century, while his maternal grandfather came from Neath. It is entirely right that players such as this should qualify for Wales and for London Welsh. It is arguable anyway that club should adopt looser qualifications than country, even though the selection of Neil Bennett over a decade ago was something of a disgrace.

But if the club do go open, they will be chucking away their principal asset. And what will they call themselves? The Old Deer, Kew Gardens or London Pagoda? There will be no prizes for suggestions.

TIME TO RETHINK THE OLD IDEAS

The Independent, December 1988

A few weeks ago I read that Bath were 'concerned' that their assistant coach, David Robson, and Tom Hudson, director of physical education at Bath University, recently went on behalf of the club to watch the Australian Rugby League touring team. The report continued: 'Any attempt by a club to improve their playing techniques by direct contact with Rugby League is in contravention of Rugby Union laws.' On Wednesday I read in this paper that John Risman, who wins his third Blue for Oxford on Tuesday, had first gained a half-Blue playing Rugby League for the university.

I then re-read a passage in Ray French's book *My Kind of Rugby*, which was first published in 1979. French wrote that interchange between the two codes was accepted as a natural part of life in the north. In south-west Lancashire, boys might have played League at the junior school up to 11, and then gone on to a secondary school to play Union to 16-18. A boy might play Union for his school on a Saturday and then League for his youth club on a Sunday. French, as an ex-League player, could coach Union at Cowley School, St Helens, while Steve Tickle, a former Waterloo captain, could coach League at another school a mile away.

It is difficult to make sense of all this, but let us try. First, there is no objection by the Rugby Union, or the unions generally, to professional sportsmen who may want to play the Union code. Peter Squires was on Yorkshire CCC's books, Dusty Hare was on Nottinghamshire's, and other examples could be cited. Second, there is no objection to amateur Rugby League. Or, if there is, the Union authorities are prepared to pass by on the other side. But, third, professional Rugby League is to be treated as a contagious disease. Hence the absurdities of the Bath club. The error of their adventurous officials, if it was an error, was to announce their presence at the Australian match in advance, and to be welcomed. If they had gone along as a couple of ordinary spectators no one would have heard anything more about it.

Even so, I cannot find anything in the laws which

specifically prohibits what they did. There is, it is true, a regulation laying down that: 'No person who is, or has been associated, in any active capacity with a non-amateur rugby club or a non-amateur rugby organisation shall participate in, or assist in, the playing, coaching, organising, controlling or administering of the game.'

But why, you may ask, was Ray French, in his pre-commentating days, permitted to coach Union? He had, after all, been a distinguished professional, having changed from Union comparatively early in his life. The answer is that he was a schoolmaster: 'A qualified teacher in full-time educational employment may be allowed to organise and coach the game within the sphere of education for which he is paid by a recognised education authority.' Presumably this means the level of education rather than the subject. Otherwise we would have the curious situation where, of two former professional League players, Mr Jones (Gym) was allowed to coach Union, whereas Mr Davies (Chemistry) was not.

Another exception is for members of the armed forces, who may play together as freely as they like. Indeed, the most impressive rugby I ever saw was in the inter-service and wartime internationals at St Helen's, Swansea, when League and Union players came together in the same side. And the outstanding player was John Risman's grandfather, Gus, more decorously known as Captain A. J. Risman (Salford).

Could those days return? I wish they would, without the intervention of a war. The two codes will never, I think, merge. The Welsh, for instance, have never taken to Rugby League, even though numerous players such as David Watkins and Lewis Jones have successfully gone north. But attempts to establish League on a regular basis in Wales have consistently failed. Yet Union sides would gain from the presence of League players. The original dispute, about broken-time, is about to be resolved, with some dissentients on the way. League has never become fully professional, as soccer has. It is now the moment for some generosity of spirit.

FAN WHO BECAME A PIONEER

The Independent, December 1988

Last Wednesday night John Morgan died. He was 59, and had been seriously ill for some three years. He was many things: a television reporter; a writing journalist; both a lover of opera and an opera librettist; an entrepreneur, in a small way of business, having been largely responsible for the setting up of the consortium which inaugurated Harlech Television.

He was also a great Welsh rugby supporter and a pioneering writer on the game. For there can be great supporters, just as there are great players. Though John relished gossip about the misdeeds of rugby's administrators in Wales – the more malicious it was, the better he was pleased – he was the most loyal and romantic of supporters. We were going to win; we always were. I remember, on the evening before the England match in February 1980, casting doubt on Wales's chances. John would have none of it. In fact it was a bad-tempered match, Paul Ringer was sent off and Wales went down 8-9. But as it was two tries to three penalties, this was a moral victory for Wales and for John. 'Alan has always been against the Welsh,' he complained to a friend of ours shortly afterwards.

He loved the trips, the travel, the whole atmosphere surrounding an international match. Here, from the book he wrote with Gerald Davies, *Side Steps*, a diary of 1984-85, is part of his account of a visit to the Paris match: 'A group from the Swansea Valley arrived in the hotel, having taken three hours to walk the one mile from the Pigalle. They thought they may have lost their way. A party from Aberavon, not feeling too well, were looking for the doctor who had come with them. They discovered he was ill in bed.' This is not at all cruel but is close to the black humour of Carmarthenshire. In fact John came from Morriston, west Glamorgan, to the east of Swansea, where his father was a builder, though the family had originally been Carmarthenshire farmers.

He was educated at Swansea Grammar School and University College, Swansea. At school he was a promising outside-half and centre, and later played for Morriston. He was close to six feet tall and powerfully built. But, with his sixth-form friend Geoffrey Nicholson, he would often go to see Swansea Town, as it was then called, on Saturday afternoons, during the marvellous days of Ivor Allchurch.

With Nicholson he wrote *Report on Rugby*, 1959. This was an innovative work; for the first time the game was treated as a social phenomenon, particularly in relation to Wales. John possessed much historical imagination, and could sympathetically recapture Imperial South Wales, when its coal kept the Royal Navy afloat and Swansea was the metallurgical capital of the world. Likewise, his rugby reports in *The Observer* in the late 1950s went beyond the game. His account of the train journey to Edinburgh is still remembered as a piece of writing. With the late H. B. Toft, *The Observer*'s correspondent after the war, he did much to raise the standard of rugby journalism. He also made several memorable television programmes with his friends of the great years, the late Carwyn James, Gerald Davies and Barry John. And he was responsible for the television film of Llanelli's win over New Zealand in 1972.

He was – there is no getting away from it, and no memoir of John would be accurate without mentioning it – something of a romancer. He once claimed to me to have played for Swansea against South Africa in 1951.

'That's funny, John,' I replied. 'I saw that match, and I can't remember you in the Swansea side.'

'I never said I actually played,' he interjected quickly. 'But I was asked to play.'

'Why didn't you, then?'

'Too scared.'

Like most of us, he would have preferred to be a rugby hero rather than the fine writer and even finer talker he actually was.

Almost 20 years after this match at St Helen's, he was to be found at the same ground, demonstrating against the same fixture. The game was called off, amid scenes of some disorder. He never thought that rugby could be separated either from politics or from life. But, as his career demonstrated, he was equally clear that, though rugby could not be separated from life, it was not the whole of life either.

CHASING WELSH DRAGON
The Independent, December 1988

As Tolstoy, who was a Russian, not a Romanian, put it: 'What then shall we do now?' Answers have ranged from sacking the selectors – always a popular solution in the Principality – to appointing Brian Thomas as team manager, or perhaps doing both. The Welsh rugby authorities, however, have a long history of spurning the creative men who are produced from time to time, roughly once in every generation. Carwyn James was never appointed national coach; had he lived, I am fairly sure he would still be standing on the touchline. As it happens, I have never been specially keen either on Brian Thomas or on the Neath club. My rugby loyalties lie further to the west. In the 1950s the Neath pack had the reputation which Pontypool acquired a couple of decades later – and which the English South-West Division enjoy, if that is the word, at present.

Neath's reputation for 'uncompromising' play was thoroughly deserved and derived from Rees Stephens's visit to New Zealand with the Lions in 1951. He brought back the gospel of hardness, but failed to inculcate the virtues of mobility and athleticism – something which Thomas has, to be fair, accomplished. Even before Stephens's time Neath were known for unnecessarily rough play. The Welsh international Dai Hiddlestone, who came from Hendy in Carmarthenshire and was Terry Price's grandfather, was considered too dirty to play for Llanelli and had to take himself off to Neath instead. Nor was Thomas an exemplar of virtue in his own playing days. There were some opponents who – quite mistakenly, of course – imagined that he had bitten them. They had clearly been overwhelmed by the ferocious expression which he would adopt to intimidate his opponents. He was not a specially quick mover, either.

Indeed, he used to lumber around the field like a superannuated tank.

No matter. Thomas is clearly the outstanding managerial figure of the decade, not only in Wales but in the whole of Britain. For this reason alone, he is unlikely to commend himself to the Welsh rugby authorities. But it is a little unfair that they should penalise his protégés as well (for, though Thomas has ceased to be the club's manager, he still takes a paternal interest in their fortunes).

Consider: Paul Thorburn was one of Wales's better players in the Samoan match and, according to my observation, was largely responsible for two of the tries scored on that occasion. His goal-kicking was wholly up to standard. Naturally, he was dropped to make way for Anthony Clement, who is an exciting footballer but no great inspirer of confidence. Thorburn then comes on as a substitute on the wing in the Romanian match. In a subsequent match for Neath as full-back, he wears the No 14 jersey 'as a joke'. Well, I like jokes as much as anybody, but these are serious matters. It is the Welsh selectors who are the joke.

Again, Jeremy Pugh is one of the most interesting props to appear for some time. In my opinion, a front row consisting of him, Ian Watkins (or Kevin Phillips) and David Young would be – not necessarily in physical, but in rugby terms – the strongest that Wales could now come up with. But Pugh suffers from being allegedly 'too small' and also from his versatility, in that he can play on either side. After an impressive first international, he was virtually discarded.

The same thing happened with Mark Jones. He is not the most refined No 8, but then neither is Dean Richards. Wales are not so strong in that position that they can afford to disregard him, particularly in view of Phil Davies's vacillating views about his natural place in the pack. Nor was Rowland Phillips playing last Saturday. There are good judges who have their doubts about his true international class. But he would undoubtedly have been an improvement on what was on display against Romania. And there is Lyn Jones, likewise 'too small', the nearest player Wales have to Andy Robinson, and, of his type, potentially the finest flanker since Haydn

Morgan. Though Neath are not my natural favourites, at least five – and possibly one or two more – of their players can justly feel hard done by.

AT ODDS WITH THE BOOKIES

The Independent, December 1988

It is hard to remember an international rugby season which England have begun with so much optimism. The bookmakers partly reflect this hope, making England second favourites at 2-1. As a professional sceptic, I wish the side well, but wonder rather whether this great good cheer is justified.

We can all list the factors that have brought it about. There were all those tries in the Irish match last season. There was the marvellous Cup final between Harlequins and Bristol. This season the leagues have fully established themselves, causing the Welsh (or some of them) to cast envious eyes across the Severn. This season, also, the Welsh, at club and at international level, have been a disappointment when they were not being a disaster. The London Division, playing under Dick Best the kind of attractive football which won Harlequins the Cup, have not only come first in the championship but beaten Australia. Above all, England have beaten Australia too.

Here let us pause for reflection. It is doubtful whether England would have defeated an Australian side playing as Australia did against Scotland later in the tour. The leagues have aroused considerable interest with bigger crowds, tables in the Sunday papers, greater 'commitment' by the players (which, in my opinion, involves too many weekly training sessions for an amateur game). But the standard of play has not been especially high.

Another, perhaps inevitable, consequence has been the devaluation of ordinary club matches. Last Saturday, for example, Wasps turned up against Rosslyn Park with only four first-choice players. An excess of the pre-Christmas

199

spirit may, I agree, have had something to do with this turn-out. But the status of the match almost certainly affected it as well. One of those who did turn out was Chris Oti. He was so swathed in bandages that he might have escaped from the Egyptian Room in the British Museum. 'Give the ball to Oti,' people said. Whereupon Rob Losowski either hung on to it or, more rarely, gave it to someone who was not Oti. Still, England have an embarrassment of talent – or anyway of speed – on the wing, though they would be in a difficulty on one side if Oti and Andrew Harriman, who are prone to injury, were crocked at the same time.

The divisional matches have followed the same pattern as the league games, only more so. They have been even more undistinguished. Observers have tended to tut-tut, to say that the players did not know one another's strange practices, or to blame the south-west for spoiling the competition with their rough ways. Well, Gloucester and Bath have never been among my favourite clubs (Bristol are a different matter). But it is a little unfair to blame the south-west when they played three matches in all in a competition of six matches. The truth is that the games in which they were not involved were perhaps not as mean in spirit but certainly as unaccomplished in execution.

Nor is this all. As far as national selection is concerned, not only does the left hand not know what the right hand is doing, but the two hands are often pulling in opposite directions. A few examples will suffice. John Buckton is back in the England squad at centre even though he was dropped by the north in favour of Brian Barley. Jamie Salmon, however, who has possibly been more responsible than any other player for London's success, is not in the squad at all. Gareth Chilcott, who is in the England squad, is left behind by the south-west, who prefer the Gloucester props. We all realise that the south-west are less a team selected on merit than a group chosen so as not to offend the three principal clubs of the area. But they are surely correct to play at No 6 John Hall, who is omitted from the England squad. They are equally right to play David Egerton in his club position at No 8 instead of trying to make him into a No 6, as England are still doing. And, as we are on injustices done to Bath players, why is Jeremy Guscott not given a chance at a higher level? And what has Nigel Redman done to offend the selectors? Bath may not be my favourite club. But I can still, I hope, be fair to them.

STEPHENS WAITING OUTSIDE
The Independent, January 1989

Hardly had I taken off for the south of France for a short break when Jonathan Davies took himself off to the north of England. Though I leave columns about What I Did On My Holidays to a famous journalist on Another Newspaper, it might nevertheless interest readers of this paper to know that William Webb Ellis is buried at Menton, on the Italian border. We came across the grave by chance while exploring the town's old cemetery. My companion (as the colour supplement traveller writers say) had never heard of him and was bored by my short exposition. The grave displays a plaque donated by the French Rugby Federation; another plaque repeats the legend that at Rugby School in 1823 Webb Ellis, in 'fine disregard' of the rules of football, picked up the ball and ran with it, so inventing rugby. I have always been somewhat sceptical of this account, and find that the *Oxford Companion to Sports and Games* (1975) shares these doubts.

Anyway, to return to the living. The departure of Davies for Widnes was accompanied by what I thought were some ungenerous comments. Perhaps he was less than wholly enthusiastic about turning out for Llanelli, but then he has been injured a good deal. Some of these injuries were brought about by his generosity – or, some would say, his foolhardiness – in playing in what were virtually exhibition matches.

Certainly he took a long time to make up his mind, but then – as he himself has been saying for nearly two years – he was subject to a lot of pressures. It would have been helpful if he

201

had made his decision last summer or at the beginning of the season, but at least Wales can start the international championship with a new outside-half in Bleddyn Bowen. We ought to thank Davies not only for winning matches but, rather more important, for providing enjoyment. And we ought to wish him the best of luck.

The most encouraging precedents for Davies are those of Bev Risman and, of course, David Watkins. Watkins, like Davies, was very fast over the first 10 yards. In fact he was, over a longer distance, the fastest member of the 1966 Lions party. Bobby Charlton once said that watching him play for Salford made him realise the meaning of true courage. We now forget that it was Watkins's departure for Salford which resolved the great Welsh outside-half controversy of that period, between him and the young Barry John. John, with his retirement at only a year older than Davies's 26, handed the succession to Phil Bennett.

The Welsh are uncomfortable when there is no clear and undisputed heir, as there is not today, and Davies cannot be blamed for this. Equally, however, the Welsh, being a disputatious people, love a good, traditional outside-half argument. At the beginning of last season, we may remember, the selectors brought in Anthony Clement, then the Swansea outside-half, at full-back. The argument was that, while Davies 'picked himself' Clement was 'too good a footballer' to be omitted from the side. Twelve months ago the natural successor to Davies was plain in view – it was Clement.

In the meantime, Bowen has been playing outside-half for Swansea and is now in the Welsh side in the same position, which is his original and his favourite one. But my feeling is that he will not last. My feeling also is that Davies's natural successor is not Clement either but another Llanelli player, Colin Stephens. At any rate, this will keep them talking happily in the tap-room for the rest of the season.

WAIL OF A TIME IN WALES

The Independent, January 1989

The principal characteristics of the season so far have been the wailing and gnashing of teeth clearly audible from my native land, and the self-congratulation verging on smugness emanating from my country of domicile. As England are not playing tomorrow, it is convenient to start with them.

We already know their team for the Scottish match. By the time the game is played, we shall have known it for close on three weeks. This is quite potty.

For one thing, England's selection should rationally have been guided by Scotland's performance tomorrow against Wales. And, for another, all sorts of misfortunes, from road accidents through strained ligaments to influenza, can befall the English players between now and then.

There is a sensible time to announce the team for an international. If it is to be played on a Saturday, the time is the penultimate Thursday before the match. This delays the choice until the last moment when a player can decide whether to turn out for his club on the preceding Saturday.

By the way, though I do not believe in premonitions, I did have the feeling that something would happen to the lock Neil Francis if he turned out for London Irish against London Scottish in the league last Saturday. So it did, and the unfortunate but imprudent Irishman is out of tomorrow's game against France.

As far as England are concerned, every moderately perceptive observer knows that Jon Webb is not of true international class (though neither, to be fair, is Stuart Thresher); that the best pair of locks in the country are still Nigel Redman and Steve Bainbridge, with Neil Edwards their closest challenger; and that John Hall is the outstanding No 6. Mike Teague's return is a credit to the principles of Samuel Smiles, but why pick yet another No 8 out of position?

About Wales's prospects I am untypically sunny. Anyone who compared and contrasted Llanelli and Neath on *Rugby Special* last Sunday with the English and Scottish matches which were shown on the same programme will have realised that here was a different kind of football, not one but several classes up. When I mentioned this to an English supporter he wittily – and, up to a point, correctly – replied that, if this was the case, it was a pity there were not more players from the two clubs in question in the Welsh side.

In fact there are seven, three from Neath and four from Llanelli, and on present club form it is Llanelli who are under-represented. Wales are appearing with five of the backs who played against Western Samoa. Though they won that match, just about, it was not a specially distinguished occasion.

But the three-quarters played rather well – notably the newish caps Nigel Davies and Mike Hall, who is out of position again tomorrow on the wing. So did Paul Thorburn. The fault lay at half-back, where Wales have a new pair and, most of all, there were faults among the forwards. Even if the latter have improved, they will find it difficult to equal the Scottish front row or the back row.

Why then do I think Wales will win? The principal reason is that, solid performer though Peter Dods is, Scotland will lack not only Gavin Hastings's place-kicking but also his abilities in counter-attack. Moreover, I repose perhaps unreasonable faith in the capacity of Jonathan Griffiths to win a match on his own.

I should love to see Ireland beat France but doubt whether it will happen. A learned commentator was writing the other day that Ireland had 'no pack' and that accordingly they needed an outside-half who 'could kick'. I cannot see the logic of that myself.

So tomorrow I shall be investing in a £10 double, on France and Wales, with another £10 on France for the championship. When someone asked André Gide who the best French poet was he replied: 'Victor Hugo, alas.' I feel just the same about the French this season.

PROFESSIONALISM DEFINED
The Independent, February 1989

In rugby, as in most other activities known to man, the same topics keep coming round like the washing-up. Thus South Africa, leagues and amateurism (real or false) have been endlessly talked about for the last decade and more. Occasionally some progress is made – or, to put it neutrally, some change occurs. But it is a slow business. On South Africa, attitudes have become firmer: it is difficult to imagine England visiting that country now, as they did as recently as 1984. On leagues, the question has been settled in England, though not yet in Wales. On amateurism, however, disparate and usually contrary opinions are flying about like, well, like fists at Sardis Road, Pontypridd.

The Bath club are proposing a kind of sunset home for old players – or, strictly, a trust fund to be distributed when players have ceased active football. From what I can make of this scheme, the people with most cause to celebrate will be the lawyers, who will surely be bringing out the vintage port in Lincoln's Inn.

Geoff Cooke, for his part, fails to see why players should not be allowed to receive cheques from publishers and bundles of banknotes from supermarkets, provided they are not paid for actually playing the game. This robust and, in my opinion, wholly defensible view has embarrassed Dudley Wood of the Rugby Football Union. There he was, on *Rugby Special* last Sunday, trying in his customary charming manner to explain away Cooke, for all the world as if he were a member of the Cabinet maintaining that one of his junior ministers had not really meant what he said.

At the same time, Brian Thomas of Neath is, I read, offering his paid services to Welsh rugby clubs as a 'consultant'. This, it appears, does not impair his continuing amateur status within the game because his job is to be a consultant. It is all great nonsense, I am afraid, and I will tell you why. The mess rugby has got itself into derives from false notions of amateurism and professionalism.

A professional is not someone who receives payment for

doing something: it is a person who earns his (or her) living substantially by the activity in question. Similarly, an amateur is not someone who receives no payment at all: it is a person who does something primarily for love. Though the derivations of words can be treacherous guides, 'amateur' comes from the Latin for 'lover'. I regard myself as a professional journalist but an amateur book writer.

Indeed, the entire discussion about the writing of books, by players and others, is based on two fallacies. The first fallacy is that the sole reason for writing a book is to make money. The second is that there is a lot of money to be made out of writing books. In fact the great Welsh players of the early 1970s did quite well for themselves from their literary activities. And, as Barry Norman likes to say, why not? Writing a book has nothing to do with amateurism and professionalism. At present, a player (past or contemporary) who is a journalist and writes a book retains his amateur status. A player who is a schoolmaster and does the same is cast into outer darkness, as Ian McLauchlan was. Yet even a supposedly professional writer, who churns out a book a year, often has to possess another source of income. On grounds of principle, the book-writing argument is easy to resolve in favour of complete freedom.

Nor do I shrink from the logic of my own definitions. Rugby League players may be paid but they are not truly professional sportsmen as players of, say, soccer, golf and tennis can be. The great majority do not earn their livings from the game. Even if Union players continue to be unpaid, I see no reason why there should not be interchangeability at every level. And so tomorrow we might be viewing Alan Tait, Martin Offiah and Peter Williams at Twickenham, and Jonathan Davies, Adrian Hadley and, possibly, David Bishop at Cardiff. Some hope! It will not happen in my lifetime, but some day it will.

PACK WHO MARCH ON BEER AND BOASTS

The Independent, February 1989

On the way to the ground, a member of the young group in front tossed a beer can over the fence into a Twickenham back garden. They all laughed at this feat. They then broke into song of a sort. The number they were attempting, 'Swing low, sweet Chariot', and the tunelessness of their rendition combined with the foulness of their prior language, clearly proclaimed them as supporters of new England. They went into the ground puffed up with the vainglorious boasting of Geoff Cooke and Will Carling – who is, it appears, to be accorded the privilege of that other former military man, the Duke of Marlborough, and appointed Captain for Life, though on Saturday's evidence with rather less justification.

Young England then sang 'God Save The Queen' with more spirit than I had ever heard before at Twickenham. They proceeded to whistle at Peter Dods when he was taking his kicks; to applaud the kicks of Jon Webb and Rob Andrew when they did not look remotely like going over; and – with more reason, it must be said – to boo Monsieur Maurette's more incomprehensible decisions, though only on that minority of occasions when they went against England.

You conclude from this that English rugby supporters are becoming more like the Welsh? Wrong: they are becoming more like English soccer supporters. Some day, mark my words, there will be a nasty incident. I am tempted to add: there certainly will be if Cooke (a manifestly decent man), Carling and their more undiscriminating admirers in the Press create unrealistic expectations among followers who – this being where they resemble not Welsh rugby supporters but English football fans – clearly have little notion of the game.

People who should know better, very different from the new, yobbish supporters of whom I write, also seem to lack any sense of history. Two years ago (though in April rather than February) Scotland came to London as a much-fancied team. England unexpectedly defeated them 21-12, Mike Harrison scoring a try, and Marcus Rose – who would almost certainly have won Saturday's match on his own – scoring a try also, two conversions and three penalties.

Two seasons later, Rose, Harrison, Jamie Salmon, Peter Williams, Richard Harding, Gary Pearce, Nigel Redman, Steve Bainbridge, John Hall and Gary Rees have been replaced by, respectively Webb, Chris Oti, Carling, Andrew, Dewi Morris, Jeff Probyn, Peter Ackford, Wade Dooley, Mike Teague and Andy Robinson. Of these, only two – Probyn and Oti – are clear gains over their predecessors. Robinson in particular had a lamentable match, actually impeding the clean release of the ball on several occasions. When he learns to think as much as he runs, he will be an international flanker.

On the way back, Young England had changed their tune to 'Cockles and Mussels'. This was not, I think, a celebration of Ireland's win in Cardiff but, rather, an indication of some mental confusion. And who shall blame them?

TWICKENHAM MANNERS
The Independent, February 1989

Since my comments in these pages four days ago on the crowd's behaviour at the England-Scotland match, several friends and acquaintances have been kind enough to say that they agreed with me. They had noticed the same deterioration themselves. One of them took his teenage son, a Watford football supporter, on his first visit to Twickenham for an international. He said that no doubt he would observe a difference from what he was used to. The boy said afterwards that, yes, they were rather better behaved at Vicarage Road.

The outward and visible signs of the new rugby hooligan are: jeans, a ski-jacket, training shoes and a can of beer. Though he will probably be wearing a scarf, it is not normally a striped supporter's scarf. Nor does he go in much for rosettes, woolly hats or other indications of team or national loyalty. The true hooligan travels anonymously and travels light. He is not invariably male. Groups of half a dozen or so young men (they tend to be in their late teens or early 20s rather than youths) often carry a complement of one or two girls of the same age, similarly attired. They do not seem to exercise much moderating influence.

On Monday I listed the following: foul language, tossing a beer can over a fence, whistling at opposing place-kickers, booing the referee and generally displaying ignorance of the game. It does not do to be priggish about these matters: for instance, I have always thought it perfectly all right to boo the referee, provided the noise is both intended and understood as an expression of informed, even if partisan, dissent.

In Saturday's match, not only were many of the French referee's decisions incomprehensible, but much of the English frustration was understandable, for John Jeffrey, Finlay Calder and Derek White spent a good part of the game offside. This, rather than any ineptitude by Dewi Morris or Rob Andrew, was the reason why the English three-quarters so often took the ball standing still. Nevertheless, I doubt whether these technical considerations moved the ski-jacketed brigade, the boring criers of 'Eng-land, Eng-land': before long we shall no doubt be treated to 'Here we go'. They had come to Twickenham to see England win, to make a lot of noise and to get as drunk as they could.

I do not look back to any mythical golden age. I remember the days when, at the old, and unreconstructed Cardiff Arms Park, the prudent man wore stout shoes and hitched his trousers well above the heel, to lessen the perils of the urine which, shortly after kick off, would trickle down the terraces like mountain streams. The England supporters of whom I write today may have drunk no more in quantity but they undoubtedly get drunker, they are younger and they know less, much less about the game than the *aficionados* of the old Arms Park, of St Helen's or, above all, of Stradey Park.

Drink is now becoming a serious problem at rugby matches. Spectators have their bags, though not their persons, perfunctorily searched as they enter the ground. Once inside, they can buy as much drink as they like – and they do. I am not puritanical about drink. *Au contraire*, as the late George Brown used to put it. But, oddly, I do not regard the

209

consumption of alcohol as part of an afternoon's rugby. I do not enjoy sipping whisky from a hipflask. At all events, the present policy of casual search and free availability afterwards is both dotty and unfair to soccer. Rugby should be treated exactly as soccer is.

THE PLAYERS ARE RESTLESS
The Independent, February 1989

I was talking to a senior England player earlier in the week. He was saying that, sooner or later, the question of payment for players had to be faced. He did not actually use the word 'professionalism'. He did not need to use it, because it did not accurately express what was in his mind. He did not – does not – want to be a professional, in the sense of a young man who earns his whole living by playing rugby. He is, as it happens, a highly intelligent chap, who is also lucky enough to have an interesting and fairly secure job.

He was perfectly prepared to put in the six or seven days or evenings a week on which the England management insist, even though this disrupted his social life. They had, he thought, no choice: in modern rugby, training of this intensity and on this scale was necessary. But he did not see why he, and others less fortunately placed, should not receive some recompense for their trouble and effort.

At the same time, players see large sums of money going into the game from commercial concerns. I am no great lover of sponsorship, especially when (as Frank Keating demonstrated in a television programme a few months ago) it deprives genuine supporters of tickets which ought to be theirs. But sports sponsorship is essentially no different from guaranteed backing and block-booking at Covent Garden. No one suggests that opera singers should not be paid. In fact they are paid a great deal, way beyond the dreams of a Jonathan Davies.

The argument is not simply that players see this money

being expended for purposes of commercial advertising and corporate public relations, and ask: why should some of it not be winging its way in our direction? Why does the RFU secretary, Dudley Wood (whom God preserve), go on so about putting money back into the game? What is this abstract entity called 'the game'? We, after all, are the game, or a good part of it, the reason why the sponsors are prepared to dish out the money in the first place.

A few years ago a well-known sports equipment company entered into an agreement with the Welsh Rugby Union to supply boots to the national team. Some members of the side objected, not so much because they were not receiving a cut of the money involved (though that certainly rankled), as because they did not care for being dictated to. Ray Williams, who was then still part of the higher echelons of the WRU, said that the players would be wearing the boots in question whether they liked it or not. A deal had been struck, a contract entered into, and the boots were as much part of the team's regulation equipment as the red jersey. When this kind of thing can happen, the sport has become professionalised – or, if you prefer the word, commercialised.

Let me draw an analogy. Even the finest hotels have, in their public areas, glass-fronted alcoves displaying expensive jewellery, bottles of scent, silk scarves, wrist-watches. No one really objects to this arrangement. Yet not even the most hard-pressed gentlemen's club would adopt or tolerate a similar arrangement, however much money there was to be made out of it. The reason is as obvious as the distinction is clear: a hotel is a commercial concern intended to make money for its shareholders, whereas a club, by contrast, is a voluntary association intended to provide for the comfort and stimulation of its own members. The hotel, in other words, is unashamedly professional; while the club is proudly amateur. Rugby Union football has long ceased being a club and is now a hotel. Unfortunately the secretary has neglected to tell the members.

THE DOUR FRENCH

The Independent, March 1989

Tomorrow's encounter between France and England is undoubtedly the match of the Five Nations championship so far. How is it, I wonder, that I feel so little affection for the sides that are involved? This is not, I may say, a matter of pro-Welsh bias. Or I do not think it is. My fellow countrymen can be intolerable when they are on a winning streak, as they were in that most remote of ages, the day before yesterday. They can even be pretty tiresome when they are on a losing streak, as they are now.

In fact my favourite national sides have always been, in no particular order of preference, France, Australia and Ireland. I like France because they have usually tried to play entertaining football. I like Australia for the same reason, and because they have to contend with rival sports in their own land. And I like Ireland because they, too, have to compete for attention in their own country, because they are prepared to have a go and, not least, because they unite Protestant and Catholic, North and South, in one side. Incidentally, this laudable union does not seem to have had the slightest effect on relations between the communities in that country. I once asked Dr Conor Cruise O'Brien why this was so. He replied that rugby was played by the middle classes, soccer by the working classes, and that 'all the trouble' came from the latter.

My emotional preference will be for Ireland over Scotland tomorrow, though I shall not be putting any money on them. Emotionally I shall be neutral between England and France, whereas in the old days I should have been firm for France. What has happened? I have not changed, but the French have. In large French towns you may now see a McDonald's hamburger dispensary among the traditional cafés and restaurants, bistros and bars. The young crowd into the new place; understandably, in a way, because they wish to seem up-to-date. Jacques Fouroux, the French coach, has brought the philosophy of McDonald's to French rugby. He preaches the gospel of success, which is to be achieved through saturation coverage, through uniformity and through bulk.

Not all Fouroux's innovations have been bad. The scrum-half's throwing the ball into the lineout often succeeds in its aim, which is to drag opposing forwards in and to secure better possession. Apart from this, the hooker (a position put into temporary cold storage by Fouroux) has quite enough on his plate already, without having to throw-in as well. Oddly enough, the French were the last country to persist with throwing-in by the wings. And many of them would still use the old-fashioned, two-handed, underarm scoop (the only kind of throw I ever mastered, and another reason for my former affection for the French).

How different it is today. And in other respects as well. Any national side that can consistently exclude backs of the class of Denis Charvet and Eric Bonneval must surely be governed more by political pressures than by rugby reason. The omission of these and other gifted players is not, however, Fouroux's chief fault, which is one of commission. French forward play was always rough and sometimes undisciplined. For robustness and occasional indiscipline, Fouroux has substituted organised brutality. I will refrain from naming names, not because I do not know them, but because among many failings of our law of libel is that foreigners can bring actions in our courts, as indeed they do.

This has nothing to do with the eight-man shove, which is a perfectly sensible piece of tactics to employ in certain circumstances – though dropping the hooker entirely, as Fouroux did until recently, raises different considerations. Nor is it a matter of laying down that only giraffes need apply for membership of the back row. No, Fouroux has coarsened and brutalised the national game. France have played attractive rugby this season, despite rather than because of him. It is good news that he will soon be relinquishing his post. Even so, I look forward with trepidation to tomorrow's match.

A TAILPIECE FOR THE UNEXPECTED
The Independent, March 1989

Jacques Fouroux is a great man in the French style. Like all such traditional characters, he is on the short side but has a fine head and a noble profile. He is authoritative (not to say authoritarian) but has his kindly, even twinkling aspects. He could play Figaro in the Mozart opera. At the very least, he ought to be a member of the National Assembly or the Mayor of Marseilles.

He seems to speak French better than his equivalents on the other side speak English. He certainly speaks English better than they speak French. However, he chose to address the Press after Saturday's match in his native tongue. He was wearing a lilac silk handkerchief in the top pocket of his dark blue blazer. On the English side such sartorial extravagance, even decadence (lilac being the colour of Oscar Wilde, always more appreciated across the Channel), would doubtless be prohibited as prejudicial to good order and rugby discipline.

M Fouroux's Press conference fell into two parts. The first, with translation provided by a friendly journalist (needless to say, a Frenchman), was attended by representatives of British and French newspapers. The second, in the French language alone, was attended by representatives of the latter group. Most of the British correspondents had loafed out beforehand. A few of us, however, decided to hang on. At the first, M Fouroux was magnanimous in defeat. Nor did he attack his own team, who were still 'great'. It had been 'a great English victory' but nonetheless 'a very good French victory'. Indeed, the French performance had been 'heroic', for they had 'never before found themselves in that position' – of having a big score piled up against them. As for the referee, M Hilditch, why, he had been 'perfect'.

During the second part, speaking to his own people, M Fouroux was still admiring of the English performance but somewhat more critical of the means whereby it had been carried out. He has, he said, no complaints about the physical commitment (*l'engagement*) displayed by the English forwards. He did, however, take exception to insults (*les insultes*) and grimaces (*les grimaces*). Perhaps he had M Teague in mind, whose response to M Robinson's try was to shake his fist in the face of M Berbizier.

Altogether, M Fouroux concluded, the French had been given a good lesson in rugby but not in British fair play (*le fair play britannique*). But then, a good politician will always tailor his words to the expectations of his audience. Or, as the great man said philosophically, several times: *Alors!*

ENGLISH DOUBLE STANDARDS
The Independent, March 1989

At the Press conference after the Scottish match, Geoff Cooke, the England coach, complained that Scotland had not allowed them to play. At the Press conference after the French match six days ago, Cooke boasted that England had not allowed France to play. Perhaps 'boasted' is too strong. There was nothing vainglorious about his approach. As a colleague in Another Newspaper put it on Monday, he might almost have been a football manager: 'We shut them out of the game, Brian, didn't we? But we got a result, didn't we, Brian?' This commentator was one of the very few who were not ecstatic about England's victory. The others were, well, over the moon.

I have no wish to strike a sour note myself. I too rejoice that Gareth Chilcott has paid his debt to society and is now a fully integrated member of the community. We all admired the athleticism which Wade Dooley and Paul Ackford displayed in the lineout. However, the count shaded in England's favour by only one in the first half and was equal in the second half. I was glad to see that Ian Robertson on *Rugby Special* confirmed my, perhaps surprising, computation. The difference lay in the higher elevation and cleaner catching shown by the English locks compared to their French equivalents – and, even more important, in the capacity of the English forwards to spoil the French possession.

As for the rest, Paul Rendall did all that was required of

215

him. Brian Moore was as active in the loose and as accurate in his throwing as he usually is. Dean Richards and Andy Robinson put the memory of the Scottish match, when they were below par, well behind them. And Mike Teague justified again the decision to play him out of position at No 6. Indeed, Teague could be challenging John Jeffrey or Philip Matthews for a Lions place.

So I am not seeking to depreciate the performance of the English forwards. What I am doing is pointing to the double standards operated by those who write about English rugby and those who organise and manage it (though not, to be fair, those who play it). This is not primarily a matter of rough play which verges on to the area of brutality, though that certainly enters into it. The complaints of the French after the match about 'insults and grimaces' and an absence of *le fair play britannique* admittedly had about them an aura of pots-and-kettles. But they had a basis in reality nevertheless.

However, the double standard is at its most marked over the method of winning, or avoiding defeat. Thus: if Scotland shut England out of the game, they are being spoilsports, whereas if England do the same to France, they are being heroes. You cannot have it all ways. That most experienced of rugby writers, Clem Thomas, is more consistent. He believes – he believed at the time – that, if England had not been over-romantic in their approach to Scotland, they would have won that match as well. But, as I say, I do not want to strike a sour note, over England or any other country. The Five Nations championship is now one of the great sporting contests of the world. With other major sports commercialised, corrupt, bad-tempered, hooligan-infested, or, in the case of boxing, plain bogus, rugby shines like a beacon. A week tomorrow, one of three countries, France, England and Scotland, could be top of the table.

My own preoccupation is slightly different. When the Lions are announced, only two Welshmen are, on present form, reasonably certain of being chosen: Robert Norster and Robert Jones. I look forward to the Cardiff match not only to provide a Welsh victory but, speaking more realistically, to supply additional names to the list of tourists.

216